Lessons
from
Ground Zero

Lessons
from
Ground Zero

Media Response to Terror

Ralph Izard and Jay Perkins
editors

Routledge
Taylor & Francis Group

LONDON AND NEW YORK

First published 2011 by Transaction Publishers

2 Park Square, Milton Park, Abingdon, Oxfordshire OX14 4RN
711 Third Avenue, New York, NY 10017

Routledge is an imprint of the Taylor & Francis Group, an informa business

First issued in paperback 2017

Library of Congress Catalog Number: 2010024457

Library of Congress Cataloging-in-Publication Data

Lessons from ground zero : media response to terror / Ralph Izard and Jay Perkins, editors.
    p. cm.
    Includes bibliographical references and index.
    ISBN 978-1-4128-1336-5
    1. September 11 Terrorist Attacks, 2001--Press coverage. 2. September 11 Terrorist Attacks, 2001, in mass media. 3. Terrorism and mass media--United States. 4. Terrorism--Press coverage--United States. I. Izard, Ralph S. II. Perkins, Jay.

HV6432.7.L45   2010
070.4'49973931--dc22

                                           2010024457

ISBN 13: 978-1-4128-1336-5 (hbk)
ISBN 13: 978-1-138-51165-1 (pbk)

Contents

Preface

It was September 11, 2001. Like the rest of the nation, faculty members in the Manship School of Mass Communication at Louisiana State University were in shock. We did not understand what had happened. We sought as much information as we could find through all available media. We wanted to know. We wanted to understand. And, since we are college faculty members, not surprisingly, we discussed the role of the news media in informing a shocked nation about one of the most tragic events in this nation's history.

In one hallway conversation in particular, a group of faculty members was in solid agreement: We believed television was doing a good job under trying circumstances. We're normally very critical, and we wondered why we had this different attitude. Why did we think the coverage was good? Then came the typical scholarly suggestion:

"We should conduct a study," Kirsten Mogensen, a visiting faculty member from Denmark, said. That was the beginning of this book. The suggestion spawned a process that at its peak involved fourteen faculty members who contributed in one form or another, four graduate students from different universities who were willing to convert their theses into chapters, a group of very cooperative professional journalists, and more than eight years since the day the idea was conceived. We solicited manuscripts and sent teams to New York, Washington, Atlanta, New Orleans, and other places to talk with people who shared these experiences and learned from them.

We confirmed what we thought we knew. This American tragedy posed challenges for journalists who initially had to work in virtual vacuums but gradually gained the information they needed to explain what happened and why it happened.

It must be said at this point that, while the focus of the analysis presented in this book involves journalism's efforts to cover a crisis, the real point is an analysis of journalism itself. We sought the qualities of good journalism. Is the answer to that question different for print and broadcast? May the strengths and weaknesses of coverage of 9/11 be generalized to journalism as a whole?

Many lessons were available to journalists as they sought to cope with the challenges of covering 9/11. The long-term question, however, is whether the answers they found would serve as catalysts for better journalism in the future, or whether they would be forgotten, put into the closet of old memories with no noticeable long-term impact on operations.

Each of the studies presented here provides part of the answers we discovered, a summary of which is presented as Chapter 1, "In the Wake of Disaster: Lessons Learned."

The result of this analysis is neither a normal scholarly book nor a standard journalistic or historical chronological accounting. It is an eclectic series of presentations that ranges from both quantitative and qualitative scholarly research to journalistic research in the form of interviews. We have done some mixing and matching, combining the scholarly work with comments from the professionals. Given the nature of both groups, it is not surprising that sometimes they agree and sometimes they disagree. But they all are thoughtful, and each provides a piece of the puzzle.

It's not over yet. Both physical and mental repairs continue to be made at Ground Zero, and the process of mourning for those lost may never end. Scholars continue their studies, and some journalists continue to seek understanding. It is our hope that this book contributes to all of these efforts.

As is the case with any project of this size, it may not be possible to recognize all of those who contributed to whatever success this book may achieve. Those people are numerous, ranging from those who physically contributed to these chapters to those who provided continuous advice, counsel, and information. We appreciate the fact that the authors of these studies were willing to submit to extensive reworking of their manuscripts. We wanted an analysis that was both meaningful and readable for a broad audience.

Others took such an active role in the process of producing this book that we must recognize them here. Thus, we share our thanks and admiration for the good work of Erin Coyle, Melody Sands, Jennifer Kowalewski, Barbara Raab, Masudul Biswas, Amy Martin, Susan Brown, Kirsten Mogensen, Laura Lindsay, Mike Beardsley, and Anne Osborne.

—RIZ and JLP

1

In the Wake of Disaster: Lessons Learned

Jay Perkins and Ralph Izard

It ranked among journalism's finest hours. That is what you heard in the weeks following September 11, 2001. The fact that you heard it often from the media themselves does not detract from the truth of the matter.

For the media did, in covering one of the biggest disasters ever to hit the United States, perform at a level far above normal, and their impressive performance did not end with the immediate impact of the catastrophe. Instead, journalists continued their analysis of what happened, the impact to property and human lives, and the impact on government and foreign relations.

Print and broadcast reporters alike looked at broader issues, especially how government performed and why it did not perform as well as was expected.

Why? What turned normally mild-mannered media into Superman and Superwoman? What changed to reconnect the nation's population to a journalistic system known to be losing readership and viewership? What did journalists learn from these experiences—and were they lessons that could be adopted or adapted to everyday news coverage?

Those were the questions on our minds as we began looking into media performance in the case of 9/11.

It would be easy to say that media performed at a high level because disasters are made for television. After all, television thrives on images, and 9/11 produced stunning images of property damage and human suffering. It also would be easy to dismiss media performance as an adrenaline surge, arguing that reporters and editors performed well because they were energized and activated by the knowledge that they were dealing with a story rivaled only by the 1941 attack on Pearl Harbor.

And it would be easy to argue that reporters connected with their audience because both were united in opposition to a common enemy. The United States had been attacked—and journalists on the scene and viewers/readers in their living rooms were affected similarly.

But those reasons, while valid, are only part of the story. Journalists also faced massive hardships in covering these events. The stories were so huge that getting a grip on them was almost impossible. While damage on 9/11 was limited to a few square blocks, the fault lines of that story extended around the world and had impact on every aspect of U.S. foreign policy.

Dispassionate Journalism Doesn't Work for Disasters

Several practices distinguished the media in their coverage of 9/11. One was that they dropped their pretense of being Olympian Gods on high, unaffected by the news, dedicated to just presenting dispassionate facts. They became, well, human. Reporters showed their emotions—at times in what they said, at other times in the expressions on their faces—on camera as well as in the columns of newspapers and magazines. Anchors in the studio and reporters on the street expressed their anger at the developments. Editors pointed out the flaws in governmental performance and demanded changes in the way government operated. And people—and eventually even some of the politicians—responded.

Another was that fair-and-balanced coverage, the mantra of reporters, gave way to advocacy reporting in which the journalists' viewpoints were clearly established. Instead of just reciting information to readers and viewers, print and broadcast reporters began providing answers and telling readers and viewers where the problems were. They began taking on a point of view and asking tough questions of politicians.

It wasn't a retreat back to the early days of American journalism—back to the opinion-only orientation of early pamphleteers—but it certainly bore similarities to the muckraking give-'em-hell attitude that journalists exhibited in the Progressive Era of the 1910s and 1920s and to the confrontational style that Edward R. Murrow exhibited during the early glory days of television.

A third practice was that journalists demonstrated that inventiveness and professionalism are the keys to crisis coverage, not logistics and prior planning. Even though all news organizations we interviewed said they had crisis coverage plans and these were important, they all admitted that nothing prepared them for the horrors of 9/11. Rather, the success of the coverage came about because reporters on the scene and producers and editors in the offices were able to overcome hurdles and work around unanticipated problems.

"Nobody had a plan for a building to come down in the heart of downtown Manhattan, let alone two of them," said CNN's John Roberts, who was a reporter for CBS News at the time.

A fourth distinguishing practice was that media acted as a consoling and reuniting mechanism in a crisis. The very act of seeing the devastation, of seeing reporters going about their jobs and politicians talking on camera, tended to reassure the audiences that things were going to be OK.

"I think journalists sometimes have a natural guilt reaction to the fact that there are people going out and helping the victims in the community," said Joe Hight, managing editor of the Oklahoman newspaper and president of the Dart Center Board. "What they don't realize is that their coverage has a dramatic effect on the community."[1]

But perhaps most significant is that the media's performance—and their ability to reconnect with the viewers and readers who, in recent years, have deserted traditional media in droves—raises important questions about where journalism is going. What does it need to do to stay relevant in this age of blogs, webcasts, and viewer self-generated media? Clearly, it cannot remain relevant by continuing to produce what Dean Mills, dean of the Missouri School of Journalism, calls "bland porridge" and what political science scholar Doris Graber calls "a boring collection of facts that the average person can't make much sense of."[2]

A More Personal Form of Journalism

Yet, the future road is unclear, and the perils are real.

The kind of journalism exhibited by all media, both during and in the aftermath of 9/11, clearly had its roots in what author Neal Gabler called the "stirring sense of righteous advocacy" that permeated the reporting of Edward R. Murrow.

"Murrow's vivid reports from wartime Europe for CBS radio brought unprecedented eloquence and immediacy to the medium. His documentaries for CBS television brought an unabashedly compassionate vision to the dispossessed and disempowered. And his famous confrontations with the red-baiting Senator Joseph McCarthy on *See It Now*, chronicled in George Clooney's acclaimed new film, *Good Night, and Good Luck,* brought courage and conscience to television news. Murrow was, as a panel on Mr. Clooney's film at the New York Film Festival put it, "the one mainstream journalist who dared 'speak truth to power.'" [3]

But Murrow left CBS News in 1961 and died in 1965. By the 1980s, righteous indignation had pretty much faded from the media landscape as media began consolidating in search of bigger profits and began preparing for the coming battle with non-mainstream media providers over the Internet. But the second part of Murrow's legacy—his innate understanding that television had to be personality driven—remained and became a stock in trade for television.

"Murrow sounded different from other journalists, too. He spoke in a rich, deep baritone that added to the dramatic effect, and he had a trademark halting cadence that turned reportage into poetry," Gabler noted. "He even looked different from the typical bedraggled reporter of 'Front Page' yore. He wore bespoke suits and always seemed to have a steely squint in his eye and a cigarette dangling elegantly from his lips or tucked into the crook of his fingers. He was dark, brooding, remote and irresistibly attractive to women—attributes more to be found in a movie star than a journalist. He had a persona.

"Murrow understood that television was a personality-driven medium, and both traded in the stock of entertainment value, which has always been the primary currency of television, including television news. Essentially, Murrow was as much entertainer as reporter."[4]

That formula of entertainer-as-much-as-reporter has characterized television since Murrow. In recent years, the entertainment portion of television, in the eyes of many, seems to have eclipsed the reporting portion. Reporting in both print and broadcast became bland, questions became less confrontational, and audiences became smaller.

That media are having trouble keeping their audiences hardly is new news. A thirty-year decline in readership of newspapers and in viewership of television has been precipitous. This trend has been fed in the past few years by new forms of self-generated media—blogs, MySpace, Facebook, YouTube, and Twitter, to name just a few—which emerged as competitors for the limited time that any audience has.

The terrorist attack of 9/11 gave journalists some respite from declining audience and decreasing importance. People tuned in—and they stayed tuned in—in great numbers. Obviously, the sheer size of the event—an attack on U.S. soil—had a great deal to do with audience interest.

Journalists and Their Emotions—Public or Private?

Coverage of 9/11 saw reporters abandoning their impassive approach to the news and showing their emotions on air. It also saw an emotional bonding between audience and reporter.

During 9/11, many reporters became citizens first, mourning with the rest of the nation, wondering why the U.S. had been attacked, investigating how it could have happened. Grief was the primary emotion, and it was an emotion shared with the nation.

This was in spite of an overriding sense that at the time permeated newsrooms across the nation that journalists should not show their emotions. When some reporters broke down on air as they stood amid the carnage of the twin towers, they represented exceptions. Part of the reason for such self-control was a feeling the nation could be headed into war—and emotion might be considered a weakness. But a huge part of the decision came because the nation badly needed consoling. News organizations decided early that the devastation should not be shown in full graphic detail. Reporters put aside personal feelings to try to seem as if they were in charge, to make it appear that things were getting back to normal. It wasn't necessarily a conscious decision, but it was done.

The enormity of the shock also impacted how much emotion was shown. Gary Tuchman, national correspondent for CNN, recalled covering a memorial service at Ground Zero. "They were so horror stricken. It was like a nightmare," he said of the mourners. But Tuchman noted that, even though many people were angry, the enormity of the shock left them no room to express that anger.

"That wasn't the first priority to be angry. It was to be grief stricken. I stood on the street corner as they arrived. Most of them, it was the first time they ever saw Ground Zero, and I just watched their faces as they saw Ground Zero for the first time. And it's like they got kicked in the stomach. It was like they got shot with a stun gun. Just watching that was incredible."

Traditional Objectivity Does Not Achieve Truth

Among the journalistic lessons of 9/11 was that these outbursts of emotion exposed a crack in American journalism's foundation. Journalists are taught to be objective. Fair and balance are their mantras. And yet journalists also are taught that they should seek the best version of the truth.

"I don't believe in fairness and balance," veteran reporter Seymour Hersh said years ago. "I believe the job of a journalist is to find the truth, and truth isn't fair and it isn't balanced."[5]

That viewpoint was shared by Jim Amoss, editor of the New Orleans *Times-Picayune*: "I've always felt that objectivity is an impossible goal and that the news is in the eye of the beholder, the beholder being a journalist," Amoss said. "So I don't like 'on the one hand, on the other hand' journalism. We have to call it as we see it and not tiptoe around the subject"

Lessons Learned for Journalism of the Future

If they're paying attention, journalists should see that many lessons are available for them in their own coverage of 9/11, and most of these questions have implications for the future of journalism and its contributions to the society it serves.

One is that it may take bigger and bigger stories to cut through the media clutter that, sadly, is American journalism—and American society—these days. The traditional media today compete with thousands of other voices. The result, as social anthropologist Thomas DeZengotita wrote shortly after 9/11, is a "clogged, anesthetized, numb" society.

"If creatures from outer space sent a diplomatic mission to the U.N., how long would it be before we were taking that in stride? (How long would it be) before Comedy Central send-ups were more entertaining than the actual creatures? About six months?

"Soap-opera politics. The therapy industry. Online communities. Digital effects. Workshops for every workplace. Viagra, Prozac, Ritalin. Reality TV. Complete makeovers. Someday, it will be obvious that all the content on our information platforms converges on this theme: there is no important difference between fabrication and reality, between a chemical a pill introduces and one your body produces, between role-playing in marital therapy and playing your role as a spouse, between selling and making, campaigning and governing, expressing and existing. And that is why we moved on after September 11, after an event that seemed so enormous, so horrific, so stark, that even the great blob of virtuality that is our public culture would be unable to absorb it. But it could. It has."[6]

Anyone with a teenager at home will agree that media have become pervasive. Every moment of our lives is now filled with them, whether newspapers, radio, television, iPods, MySpace, Facebook, YouTube, or Twitter. We have at our fingertips the ability to read hundreds, if not thousands, of mainstream newspapers daily from around the globe. We have at our fingertips the ability to watch recorded television newscasts from other countries, to bundle our favorite television show for watching while walking, to timeshift media we don't have time to watch into another spot in our busy schedules.

The result is that much of what is seen and heard is ignored because so much is available to see and hear. A story such as 9/11, which shook our faith in our future, can break through this media clutter because it has intense relevance.

A third lesson is the powerful fact that the media play critical roles in reassuring the population during a disaster even if journalists claim consolation is not part of their agenda. The very fact that people may be seen going about their jobs in a normal manner, interviewing officials, talking to fire fighters, is reassuring to a population worried about its future. That was seen in 9/11 with hundreds of residents citing the coverage of local media as helping them get through the disaster.

The media not only were sources of information for citizens during these disasters; they also were sources of information for government. Television had live cameras on the scene in New York as 9/11 unfolded. Their pictures and commentaries were important sources of information for government leaders in Washington and state capitals. The cameras provided access to information that agents in the field could not provide—and the cameras did so dispassionately, without the filters of human intelligence.

"I think they were relying on the networks for information, not just the networks, everybody. They rely on cable and everyone," said Paul Salvin, executive producer for ABC *World News Tonight*. "That's not that unusual. Very often the government is relying on our information for things, as they should. You know why? We're good information gatherers."

The bottom line is that journalists have leadership roles in today's media-dominated world, whether they like it or not. And those who would have media remain on the sidelines, as impassive non-participants, do not understand the changing nature of the world.

A fourth lesson is that planning is both necessary and important, but inventiveness and intelligence are far more necessary in the end. Journalists will find a way to ferret out accurate information when government cannot or will not provide it. Government officials accounted for only about 20 percent of all sources used in the opening hours of 9/11. Part of that could be attributed to the fact that much of government was in hiding, waiting to see if other attacks were planned. Part of it could be attributed to the fact that journalists knew from past experience that the Bush administration was not particularly helpful in passing on useful information. And part of it was the efforts of governments in New York and Washington to control what information was available to journalists.

Reporters quickly learned in 9/11 that government was as clueless as they were. "An interesting thing on that day, nobody knew," said Brian Kennedy, national desk, ABC News. "I mean a lot of people we talked to on the phone, officials, they didn't know what was going on. And they tried to tell you as best they could. One of the things I remember from that day was that people would tell you things, and they were just flat wrong."

The media response was to find other avenues and other sources. Reporters barred from Ground Zero found ways to get in. Correspondents who found no officials who could or would speak to the issue found other sources who would talk. Technology also played a role in that the Internet gave reporters quick access to information such as flight schedules, number of seats on an airplane, maintenance records and so forth.

A fifth lesson is that the long-standing belief in "accuracy, accuracy, accuracy" does not lose its importance in the midst of chaos. Indeed, it's even more important. The major media function in a crisis is to provide clear, precise, accurate, and timely information to thousands of people who must make decisions about their own safety. Often, there can be no margin of error.

Finally, the experiences of 9/11 reinforced what good journalists know already: Their job is big; it's more than witnessing and describing. It's an intellectual exercise, and journalists serve different functions at different times. If they're on top of their jobs, coverage begins before the crisis because they've done their homework and they know what is possible. They issue warnings, not specifically possible for 9/11, but certainly possible in a broader sense given the trends of worldwide societies these days.

When something does happen, their principal task is to collect facts about what happened and provide that information to both the public and officials. They advise citizens about what to do and deal with relief and recovery efforts as that information becomes available. As the cleanup begins, they open discussions of lessons learned for the future and begin an analysis of broader implications.

It is this latter need—analysis of what such an event means in the broader context—that often is forgotten by journalists with short attention spans and news organizations that focus only on the immediate crisis before moving on to the next. But 9/11 did not permit such negligence. The story of the terrorist attacks extended around the world in the form of a "War on Terror."

Journalism Must Adapt to the Changing World

It was A. J. Liebling, noted journalist and media critic, who said years ago "freedom of press belongs to those who own one." But almost everyone owns a press today. Anyone with a computer and an Internet connection today can be—and is—a journalist. Anyone with a computer and an Internet connection can influence more people today than Thomas Payne ever thought about in the early days of the American Revolution.

That means mainstream media are going to have to adapt to this changing world in which anyone can speak his or her mind and many do with more force and a point of view. Traditional journalists did so in their coverage of 9/11. Yet, if they retreat back to the old standard of presenting two sides to every story, as if every story had exactly two sides that were 180 degrees removed, and if they continue to concentrate on buildings, automobiles, and other inanimate objects instead of the real lives of real people, mainstream media will continue to lose their relevance.

"Power is moving away from journalists as gatekeepers over what the public knows," said the Pew Research Center in 2005. "Citizens are assuming a more active role as assemblers, editors and even creators of their own news. Audiences are moving from old media such as television or newsprint to new media online. Journalists need to redefine their role and identify which of their core values they want to fight to preserve—something they have only begun to consider."[7]

Geneva Overholser, a former New York Times columnist and now director of the School of Journalism at University of Southern California's Annenberg School for Communication, is one who believes continued reliance on dispassionate delivery will not work.

"The commitment to being dispassionate often felt to consumers like a lack of concern. Disinterest came across as uninterested—and uninteresting. More and more, Americans are trusting the information they get from sources with a 'voice,' including comedy programs like *The Daily Show*, documentaries like *An Inconvenient Truth* or theater like *Stuff Happens*, and FOX News's remarkable growth stems in significant part from its clear point of view."[8]

Neither, says former New York Times reporter Doug McGill, will continued reliance on concepts such as objectivity and fairness and balance work when the audience demands more direction.

"For more than a century," he said, "objectivity has been the dominant professional norm of the news media. It has at its heart the noble aim of presenting indisputable facts upon which everyone in society can agree, and build upon toward the goal of a better society. Unfortunately, the ideal of objectivity has in practice in today's newsrooms become a subtle but powerful means of self-censorship. It's a conglomeration of contradictory practices that serve the purpose of rationalization as often as investigation. It has become a crutch for journalistic practices that work against civic aims."[9]

Michael Kinsley, editor of Slate Magazine, argues that objectivity has outlived its usefulness and predicts it will soon vanish from American journalism.

"Objectivity is not a horse to bet the network on. Or the newspaper either," he said. "No one seriously doubts anymore that the Internet will fundamentally change the news business. The uncertainty is whether it will change only the method of delivering the product or will also change the nature of the product. Will people want, in any form, a collection of articles, written by professional journalists from a detached and purportedly objective point of view? Or are blogs and podcasts the cutting edge of a new model—more personalized, more interactive, more opinionated, more communal, less objective?

"It might even be a healthy development for American newspapers to abandon the conceit of objectivity. This is not unknown territory. Most of the world's newspapers, in fact, already make no pretense of objectivity in the American sense. But readers of the good ones (such as *The Guardian* or the *Financial Times* of London) come away as well informed as the readers of any 'objective' American newspaper."[10]

The Need to Supersede Journalistic Tradition

On the surface, much may be said in favor of abandoning traditional objectivity—even fairness in some special cases—as a goal. The public knows, even if the media refuse to acknowledge, that the art of newsgathering and storytelling is inherently unfair and that all accounts are biased by reporters' and editors' perspectives. The public knows that FOX is more conservative than CNN, that the *New York Times* is more liberal than the *Wall Street Journal*. And the knowledge that journalism refuses to be honest in this regard clearly has impact in the negativity and lack of trust in media shown by poll after poll in recent years.

Likewise, the journalistic pretense that the facts speak for themselves does not serve readers, viewers, and listeners. This is not a new idea. More than 60 years ago, the Hutchins Commission argued: "It is no longer enough to report the fact truthfully. It is now necessary to report the truth about the fact."[11]

What has happened is that the media have gone overboard in their definition of objectivity and even fairness. Objectivity should never have been defined as pretending one has no opinions or no feeling. It does not mean automatic balance of extreme ideas that lacks clarity, and perhaps even distorts real meaning. It does not mean the ridiculous gets equal attention to the legitimate. Rather, objectivity and fairness are efforts to be realistic, to provide human context, to be broad in dealing both with facts and with human disagreements or perceptions. And, in journalism, they mean respecting the intelligence and feelings of those in the audience by not assuming they do not understand or care.

But journalists, of course, need to hang out the caution sign. Abandoning such traditional concepts may well be trading one set of problems for another, especially if journalists go again to the extreme. For the problem may not be objectivity or fairness but overemphasis on impact. The problem may be journalism's panic over the need to distinguish one story from another, one newscast from another, one anchor from another in this media-saturated society.

Gabler makes the point clearly in his discussion of Murrow's legacy. "If a line runs from Murrow to Peter Jennings, Tom Brokaw and *Nightline*, it also runs to Bill O'Reilly, Chris Matthews and *The Barbara Walters Specials*. They are all Murrow's heirs, not because they speak truth to power or because they are guided by conscience or because they adhere to any high-minded principle as he did. They are Murrow's heirs because they all demonstrate an understanding that stardom matters, that news without dramatic form isn't likely to survive."[12]

Former British Prime Minister Tony Blair, who spent years sparring with the decidedly partisan and hardly "fair-and-balanced" British press, made the same point in a speech to news executives only days before he stepped down as prime minister.

Blair said British media were impacting adversely on public life and blamed the speed at which they now must operate and the increased competitive pressure caused by new forms of media as the culprits.

"The media world—like everything else—is becoming more fragmented, more diverse and transformed by technology. The news schedule is now 24 hours a day, 7 days a week. It moves in real time."

The result, Blair argued, is that media reporting today "to a dangerous degree is driven by impact. Impact is what matters. It is all that can distinguish, can rise above the clamor, can get noticed. Impact gives competitive edge. It is this necessary devotion to impact that is unraveling standards, driving them down.... The audience needs to be arrested, held and their emotions engaged. Something what is interesting is less powerful than something that makes you angry or shocked."[13]

That may be the real lesson of 9/11. The media performed well in this disaster because the disaster had so much emotional impact that it could easily accommodate the impact that often is artificially added by anchors and correspondents. In other circumstances, impact that causes media to seek out and focus on the absurd, on the flaws of human nature, on the deviations of humankind, was perfectly normal in a disaster setting. No need compelled hyping a celebrity's indiscretions, a parent's anguish, a politician's hypocrisy.

No need existed to make the story big. Viewers could see the twin towers collapsing, the people running from the massive cloud of dust and smoke.

In the chaos of covering 9/11, journalists relied on their training and instincts. At times this carried them beyond traditional objectivity into a style of journalism that was ultimately human. It was not designed to satisfy the requirements of a dispassionate form of past years. It was to meet the needs of those in their audiences.

Perhaps the early twenty-first century did produce journalism's finest hour. Perhaps it provided a guided path for media to evolve into a more advanced and useful creature. The issue—indeed, the challenge—is whether, when the stories are not so dramatic, journalists can learn those lessons, and whether the product of their work can become real, can become relevant.

Notes

1 . Haynes, M. (2006, December 22). A Tragedy's Emotional Impact Can Engulf Journalists, *Pittsburgh Post-Gazette*, Pg. E1.
2. Overholser, G. (2006). On Behalf of Journalism: A Manifesto for Change. Retrieved on September 1, 2007, from *http://www.annenbergpublicpolicycenter.org/Overholser/20061011_JournStudy.pdf*.
3. Gabler, N. (2005, October 9). Good Night, and the Good Fight, the *New York Times*, pg. 12.

4.   Gabler, N. (2005, October 9). Good Night, and the Good Fight, the *New York Times*, pg. 12.
5.   Hersh, S. (1985, Sept. 17). Speech to journalism students, Louisiana State University.
6.   de Zengotita, T. (2002, April). The Numbing of the American Mind: Culture as Anesthetic, *Harper's Magazine*, Retrieved September 8, 2007, from *http://www.csubak.edu/~mault/Numbing% 20of%20american%20mind.htm*.
7.   Pew Research Center (2006, March 14). State of the News Media: Tough Times for Print Journalism - and In-Depth Reporting, Pew Research. Retrieved on April 13, 2008, from *http://pewresearch.org/ pubs/213/state-of-the-news-media*.
8.   Overholser, G. (2006). On Behalf of Journalism: A Manifesto for Change.
9.   "Our Code is Falling to Pieces: Doug McGill on the Fading Mystique of an Objective Press," in *PressThink*, 2004. *http://journalism.nyu.edu/pubzone/weblogs/pressthink/2004/10/29/mcgill_essay.html*.
10. Kinsley, M. (2006, April 7). The Twilight of Objectivity; Lou Dobbs Might be a bit Overheated but the New Media Direction is Clear, *Pittsburgh Post Gazette*, pg. B7.
11. Commission on Freedom of the Press (1947). *A Free and Responsible Press*. Chicago: University of Chicago Press, 22.
12. Gabler, N. (2005, October 9). Good Night, and the Good Fight, the *New York Times*, pg. 12.
13. Blair, T. (2007, June 12). Lecture by the Prime Minister, The Right Honorable Tony Blair, MP, on Public Life, *Reuters*. Retrieved on April 13, 2008, from *http://image.guardian.co.uk/sys-files/Politics/documents/2007/06/12/BlairReustersSpeech.pdf*.

2

From Chaos to Mourning: The Case of CNN

Kirsten Mogensen

CNN likes to tout itself as the network people watch in a crisis. That certainly was the case on 9/11.[1] The situation during the first 24 hours of the attacks was unique, and so was the role of national television that day and night when the nation felt panic, shock, anger, and insecurity—and remained glued to the television screen.[2]

Opinion polls showed that most Americans were satisfied with 9/11 coverage.[3] The journalists generally were proud of the coverage, according to trade journals as well as this project. But national television coverage on September 11 also has been criticized by several intellectuals, who blamed the media for not asking "why" the terrorists attacked the U.S., for bringing incorrect information, for rallying around the flag and President Bush[4] and for not being objective and balanced.[5] While such critiques may be relevant, the discussions will take on additional meaning only if they are based on comprehensive knowledge of what television actually told its viewers that day.

This project was concentrated on the first 24 hours of coverage during which the public was in a state of crisis. According to sociologist Arthur G. Neal, "An extraordinary event becomes a national trauma under circumstances in which the social system is disrupted to such a magnitude that it commands the attention of all major subgroups of the population.... The major task, individually and collectively, is that of integrating the traumatic event into the fabric of social life in order to make it less threatening."[6]

When the social order is seriously disrupted, the public usually will desire as much information as the media can provide. Incomplete information at a time of crisis leads to suspicion and rumor.[7] Violence sometimes erupts when the public is sad and angry at the same time.[8] However, if people can easily determine from the media the degree of danger present, behavior tends to be less extreme.[9] During a crisis, television provides not only facts and meanings but offers a kind of therapy to viewers,[10] and it functions as a ready medium for government officials who need to address the public.[11] [12]

Previous research has lumped crisis coverage into three stages,[13] but this study found five distinct stages within CNN's coverage during the first 24 hours of 9/11: [14]

1. *The catastrophe*: Chaos and horror. 8:49 a.m. to approximately 6:40 p.m.
2. *Control and national unity*. Approximately 6:40 p.m. to 9:10 p.m.
3. *Rescue work*. Approximately 9:10 p.m. to 12:30 a.m.
4. *International*. Approximately 12:30 a.m. to 6 a.m.
5. *Mourning begins*. Approximately 6 a.m. to 8:49 a.m.

In addition, coverage emphasis changes even within each of the five segments. For example, a content analysis of the September 11 coverage of CNN, CBS, ABC, NBC and FOX News showed that the emphasis changed even within the first eight hours. From 8:45 a.m. to 11 a.m., the coverage was devoted mostly to descriptions of the disaster; from 11 a.m. to 3 p.m. the description of what happened declined while coverage of U.S. government reactions and the severity of the disaster increased; and after 3 p.m. the severity of the disaster and safety concerns were in focus.[15]

Coverage, of course, included overlapping themes and sources as well as replays of footage from one stage to the next. However, the stages of CNN coverage differ with regard to three important aspects: major *events,* including the public debate; the type of *sources* giving interviews and public statements; and the degree to which journalists in a given stage covered *events staged by government* officials or seemingly chose to show more independent work.[16]

Stage One: Catastrophe, Chaos and Horror

The first stage of 9/11 coverage was characterized by chaos, uncertainty, and abnormality. Journalists, in the absence of official information, did a major part of their research while broadcasting, often just ad libbing to the pictures. CNN anchor Carol Lin is typical of much of the coverage during this stage:

> This is just in. You are looking at obviously a very disturbing live shot there. That is the World Trade Center, and we have unconfirmed reports this morning that a plane has crashed into one of the towers of the World Trade Center. CNN Center right now is just beginning to work on this story, obviously calling our sources and trying to figure out exactly what happened. (CNN, 8:49 a.m.)

While the initial events were unfolding, coverage was characterized by a general lack of security, leadership, and overview. The country's political leadership flew to secure locations, the economic leadership flew from the burning World Trade Center, and even the rescue workers flew from the scene of disaster. Much of the national administration closed down, buildings—such as the Justice Department, the State Department, the Congress, the White House and the UN—were evacuated, the stock market was suspended, airports and the national railways closed.

CNN showed events unfolding: American Airlines Flight 11 departed Boston for Los Angeles, was hijacked and crashed into the North Tower of the World Trade Center at 8:45 a.m. United Airlines Flight 175 departed Boston for Los Angeles, was hijacked and crashed into the South Tower of the World Trade Center approximately 18 minutes later. The South Tower collapsed in a plume of ash and debris at approximately 10 a.m., and as people ran for their lives, the North Tower collapsed at 10:27 a.m., followed by other buildings such as building 7, a 47+-story structure which collapsed at 4:20 p.m.

American Airlines Flight 77 departed Washington Dulles for Los Angeles, was hijacked and crashed into the Pentagon at 9:43 a.m. United Airlines Flight 93 departed Newark for San Francisco, was hijacked, and crashed in Shanks Ville, Pa., at 10:10 a.m. Late in the afternoon, viewers were given the first name of one of the airplane passengers who had been killed. That was Barbara Olson, a former commentator on CNN, who had called her husband from United Airlines Flight 93 knowing it had been hijacked.

As this was occurring, CNN interviewed witnesses about what happened or what they thought had happened. Eyewitnesses told how some people had jumped from upper stories to escape the searing heat of the blaze (CNN, 10:27 a.m.). CNN named its special coverage *America Under Attack* (CNN, 10:58 a.m.) and at least every hour the audiences received an overview of the day's events.

After noon came the first reports about the valuable efforts of rescue workers during the evacuation of buildings (CNN, 12:16; 3:21 p.m.), and shortly after it was confirmed that many police officers and fire fighters had been trapped in the buildings. President Bush thanked the rescue workers in a public statement (CNN, 1:12 p.m.) and soon fire fighters were called "brave" (CNN, 1:40 p.m.)—a term that would follow the profession in the months to come.

For security reasons, President Bush was flying around the country, and CNN said it would not tell the viewers where he had been until he had left (CNN, 1:30; 2:22 p.m.). Congressional leaders also moved to secure locations (CNN, 3:28 p.m.). However, New York's Mayor Rudy Giuliani and Governor George Pataki were not in hiding. They were on the streets in New York, close to the WTC site, where Giuliani at one time was trapped in the debris (CNN, 12:28 p.m.), and they briefed the press (CNN, 11:01 a.m.; 2:36; 3:55 p.m.).

The first international reaction was broadcast shortly after noon on CNN, and it was a Taliban spokesman who denied that Osama bin Laden had anything to do with the attacks (CNN, 12:25; 12:50 p.m.). Then came condolences from Palestine's leader Yasir Arafat, shown with footage of Palestinians celebrating in the street (CNN 3:38 p.m.) and from Israel. In the early evening, CNN broadcast live from Kabul in Afghanistan, where explosions occurred.

The journalists speculated these might have been caused by American retaliation. The live coverage lasted for 37 minutes and stopped when the president, from his secure location, announced that those explosions had nothing to do with U.S. retaliation, but were part of a civil war in Afghanistan (CNN, 5:57 to 6:34 p.m.). At this time, it also was announced that all international flights had arrived safely (CNN, 5:45 p.m.), and the president was on his way to Washington (CNN, 6:34 p.m.)

While most attention was given to the unfolding events, CNN also offered a medium for experts, decision makers, politicians, and intellectuals to start a political debate about the implications of the events and try to make sense of what was happening. It is interesting to note that a large percentage of those participating in the discussion had "former" as part of their titles. Many had once played important roles in national as well as international politics, but on 9/11, they were not key players.

Among these were four former secretaries of state: Henry Kissinger, Lawrence Eagleburger, James Baker, and George Schultz. They were joined by former U.S. envoy Richard Holbrooke and by a number of men previously in charge of the nation's security such as former NATO

Commander Gen. Wesley Clark, former National Security Adviser Samuel Berger, former Secretary of Defense William Cohen, former CIA Director Robert Gates, and former Assistant FBI Director James Kallstrom.

Seen from a viewers' point of view, it was to a large extent that these former officials—together with a dozen members of the Congress, two Israeli ministers and authors Tom Clancy and Peter Bergen—initially constructed what may be called the *American discourse,* with CNN journalists as discussion leaders.

The major questions discussed during the first ten hours were: What are we witnessing? How do we retaliate? What was wrong with our security system?

1. What Are We Witnessing?

A few minutes after United Airlines Flight 175 crashed into the South Tower, former National Transportation Safety Board spokesman Ira Furman stated that the incidences most likely were not accidents. Twenty minutes later, President Bush, in his first public reaction, said: "Terrorism against our nation will not stand" (CNN, 9:31 a.m.). After that point, the events generally were referred to as terrorism. After noon came the early interpretations. Republican Senator Orrin Hatch talked about an international Jihad against the West, and Republican Senator John McCain said this was obviously an act of war (CNN, 12:35 p.m.). Republican Representative Curt Weldon labeled the events a twenty-first-century war, and former National Security Adviser Samuel Berger said that whoever did it had declared war on the United States.

But what type of war was it? The terrorist attacks were first compared to the Dec. 7, 1941, attack on Pearl Harbor. As the discussion continued, however, agreement emerged that this war clearly was different from previous wars, and discussions were held of the characteristics of this new type of warfare. Wesley Clark talked about an era in which global communications make it impossible for one nation alone to deal with international terrorism, and Israeli Prime Minister Ariel Sharon talked about an international war against all terror groups, which led Wesley Clark to discuss how the United States deals with international terrorist organizations.

Another issue was what the terrorists wanted. No organization had claimed responsibility, so the experts tried to reach an understanding based on analyses of the signs of the events. Journalists and commentators quickly noted that the terrorists had attacked buildings symbolizing

U.S. military and economic power, but the question "why?" remained to be answered. James Kallstrom said the terrorists hated the American lifestyle, and since it seemed as if the war was about different world-views, Israeli Foreign Minister Shimon Peres talked about a need for cooperation among religions against terrorism and suicide terror. Author Tom Clancy mentioned religious terrorism and suicide terror in other parts of the world, including Northern Ireland.

2. How Do We Retaliate?

Parallel to the dialogue about the definition, another discussion emerged about how the United States should respond. In his statement at 9:30 a.m., President Bush made it clear that the government would "conduct a full-scale investigation to hunt down and to find those folks who committed those acts." The first problem naturally was who was behind the attacks, and Wesley Clark opened that discussion with comments about bin Laden (CNN, 11:30 a.m.). During the following debate, a few other potential suspects were mentioned but quickly forgotten. By 12:40 p.m., CNN was quoting Orrin Hatch as saying the U.S. intelligence community believed the attacks reflected bin Laden's signature. The magnitude of the events, the sophistication of the attacks, the knowledge of bin Laden's organization, and the potential scope of retaliation quickly led to an agreement among the participants about the need for international cooperation.

If bin Laden was behind the attacks, the next question dealt with whether Afghanistan should suffer, or more precisely: Are countries that harbor or support terrorism responsible for terrorist acts? Richard Holbrooke said countries that hide terrorists should be held equally responsible (CNN, 1:04 p.m.), and he gained support for this view. However, would it be acceptable to kill innocent Afghans or to retaliate against terrorist groups such as bin Laden's before they were proven guilty? In other words: How about justice in the new war?

It was late afternoon when Wesley Clark referred to the risk of retaliation against innocent people, and this led to additional discussion during the following hours. Lawrence Eagleburger said the United States should not hesitate too long with investigation and court processes, so that the retaliation would come too late for its meaning to be clear, while William Cohen said the United States would not be indifferent about how many innocent people were killed. He said that was precisely the difference between the terrorists and United States.

When CNN later in the afternoon reported explosions in Kabul, the interviewees refused to comment on it before President Bush had sent the message that those explosions were not part of a U.S. retaliation.

3. What Was Wrong with Our Security System?

As Americans watched the attacks on New York and Washington, DC,, they naturally asked how this could happen in a highly-developed democratic country with the world's strongest military. The question was raised several times during the day, but most of the interviewees refused to accuse U.S. institutions of misconduct and answered critical questions in diplomatic terms, often adding that the FBI and CIA needed more resources.

Approximately 45 minutes after the first attack on the World Trade Center, CNN Correspondent David Ensor implied a problem when he said: "U.S. intelligence officials say they had no warning of anything like this coming along." According to a London-based Arab journalist, followers of bin Laden had warned three weeks earlier that they would carry out a huge and unprecedented attack on U.S. interests; however, they did not specify what it was, and author Peter Bergen implied that bin Laden had actually sent a warning in a videotape floating around the Middle East in which he called for attacks on the United States (CNN, 1:15 p.m.).

During the first stages, critical questions were asked about the performance of the CIA and the FBI by at least two Washington correspondents, David Ensor and Kate Snow, and four anchors—Judy Woodruff, Aaron Brown, Jeff Greenfield, and Paula Zahn.

Stage Two: Control and National Unity

The second stage started at 6:40 p.m. when President Bush returned to the White House and ended at approximately 9:10 p.m., when the national leadership in Washington withdrew from the public spotlight after a long, stressful day. This stage is a contrast to the first stage because these hours were used for a massive proclamation of leadership and control.

Government officials, including the president, cabinet members, and members of the Congress, staged televised events such as press briefings, the president's speech to the nation, and a symbolic gathering of members of the Congress on the steps to the Capitol. Without exception, government officials and politicians promised to unite behind the president. They referred to national symbols and values and talked about the strength of the nation. Within two hours, most of the major political leaders appeared on television seemingly strong and ready to look forward.

CNN showed a marine helicopter land on the South Lawn of the White House and President Bush peacefully left the flight, crossed the lawn and entered the Oval Office (CNN, 6:57 p.m.). Defense Secretary Donald Rumsfeld and senior military officials held a press conference in the part of Pentagon that had not been destroyed by the terrorist attack. In the White House, Attorney General John Ashcroft, Transportation Secretary Norman Mineta and HHS Secretary Tommy Thomson held a similar televised press briefing. On the steps of the Capitol, Republican House Speaker Dennis Hastert and Senate Democratic Majority Leader Tom Daschle said they stood united behind the president.

After these statements of unity, members of Congress spontaneously sang *God Bless America* (CNN, 7:24 p.m.). However, the situation was still not normal. Schools and the stock exchange in New York closed the following day (CNN, 8:40 p.m.), and along the borders of United States U.S. navy ships sailed to signal that America was the strongest military in the world (CNN, 7:42 p.m.). It was announced that the UN would meet the following day to discuss a response.

The president talked to the nation (CNN, 8:31-8:36 p.m.), and before he spoke, the symbolic meaning was pointed out to the viewers by Anchor Aaron Brown and Senior White House Correspondent John King:

Aaron Brown: There are, it seems to us, moments in a president's term, the Challenger for President Reagan, the Gulf War for President Bush, Oklahoma City for President Clinton. Now this, when a country looks to a president for information and reassurance. Our senior White House correspondent, John King, I expect, will hear both today.

John King: Expect you will, Aaron, on a day defying description. The president, we are told, wants to deliver a message of "resolve and reassurance to the American people." Mr. Bush, back at the White House now for a couple of hours. He has been briefed by the vice president and members of his national security team. The key members of the Bush cabinet here, as well, trying to direct the federal government's response to this crisis. Mr. Bush will address the American people, as you mentioned from the Oval Office here at the White House, after a day that began in Florida, saw him to go to a military installation in Louisiana, then a second military installation in Nebraska, all this as he tried to stay in touch with the national security team. And all this, as the White House, the Secret Service, and the military decided whether or not it was safe to bring the president back to Washington. They very much wanted the political statement of the president returning to the White House, to try to dispel any notion that this was a country under siege. Still, this is a key defining moment for this president, eight months into office. We're just a few minutes away from hearing him on this day of tragedy in the United States, address the American people from the Oval Office.

Brown: And indeed, that political message that the government is functioning despite all that's happened, was repeated again and again by officials in Washington. Late today, I remember hearing Karen Hughes. It was almost the first thing she said. She was reassuring the American people that their government is running, despite it all. This is the government continuation plan in the textbooks in Washington, D.C. This is a very young administration. And this is a major test, John.

King: That's right, Aaron. And at times, there is a conflict, if you will, between the security arrangements and the political calculations. The president being kept out of Washington, the key leaders in Congress being taken to a secure bunker outside of Washington, all that part of a protocol. (CNN transcript)

President Bush's speech to the nation from his Oval Office lasted less than five minutes and, among other things, he said:

Thousands of lives were suddenly ended by evil, despicable acts of terror. The pictures of airplanes flying into buildings, fires burning, huge structures collapsing have filled us with disbelief, terrible sadness, and a quiet, unyielding anger. These acts of mass murder were intended to frighten our nation into chaos and retreat, but they have failed. Our country is strong.... America was targeted for attack because we are the brightest beacon for freedom and opportunity in the world, and no one will keep that light from shining. Today, our nation saw evil, the very worst of human nature, and we responded with the best of America. With a daring of our rescue workers, with the caring for strangers and neighbors who came to give blood and help in any way they could.... The functions of our government continue without interruption.... The search is under way for those who are behind these evil acts. I've directed the full resources of our intelligence and law enforcement communities to find those responsible and to bring them to justice. We will make no distinction between the terrorists who committed these acts and those who harbor them.... America and our friends and allies join with all those who want peace and security in the world, and we stand together to win the war against terrorism.... None of us will ever forget this day; yet we go forward to defend freedom and all that is good and just in our world. (CNN Transcript)

After the presidential speech, Cardinal Roger Mahony, archbishop of Los Angeles, advised parents to gather their families, light candles and talk about the events of the day in relation to the holy scriptures of whatever religion they had (CNN 8:41 p.m.). He was the first religious leader interviewed on CNN.

At the World Trade Center, it was still not possible to start a full-scale rescue operation because the fires made it dangerous to enter the buildings. CNN said approximately 200 fire fighters and 78 police officers were missing—many assumed dead during their rescue work. At the end of this stage, New York Governor Pataki told the press that equipment had been brought into the area, so that the rescue operation could start.

Stage Three: Rescue Work

When chaos began to gain some structured response, the rescue work came into focus in the third stage from approximately 9:10 p.m. to 12:30 a.m. Even though the fires at the World Trade Center would continue for days, the situation was now such that the rescue work could start, and CNN broadcast live from the site so that the viewers could see this response occurring.

Now some people, who earlier in the day had fled in panic and were covered by debris, participated in CNN's popular *Larry Ling Live*. They sat in the studio telling their stories. They were clean, well-dressed, orderly and controlled. The attacks and all the fear could be discussed in past tense. They told about the brave rescue workers and cooperation among people on their way down, but also about fire fighters coming up the stairs with heavy loads, collapsing and blocking the way for people on their way down (CNN, 9:13 p.m.). One of the interviewees showed a picture of a missing person. He was the first to do so on CNN. In the days to come, many relatives would follow his example and bring photos of their loved ones to reporters on the streets of New York and Washington, D.C.

Mayor Giuliani and other government officials held a press conference in which they listed the names of some of the fire fighters who had died in the World Trade Center (CNN, 9:58-10:13; 11:30-11:47 p.m.). Shortly after, CNN told about some of the flight passengers who had died. A mother of one of the flight victims told the viewers how her son had called her from the flight that crashed in Pennsylvania. In the end, relatives were provided phone numbers, web pages, and e-mail addresses from which they could obtain information about the now more than 300 missing fire fighters, hundreds of flight passengers, and thousands of other presumed victims. It was now clear that some American Muslims feared retaliation, and Giuliani asked Americans not to retaliate against American Muslims (CNN, 10:08 p.m.).

The passenger lists contained some clues about whom the hijackers might be. The FBI started investigations in Florida where some of the hijackers had attended flight schools. A few men were detained for questioning in New York. Originally, it was said that they were carrying explosives in their car, but that was not the case, and the information was corrected three minutes later (CNN, 11:29; 11:33 p.m.). Attention also was given to security concerns at airports, and CNN told its viewers that several investigations had shown problems with security at the airport in Boston where two of the flights were hijacked.

For the first time, CNN showed long-distance shots of people jumping from the World Trade Center Towers—or at least it was first time viewers were told what they saw were people jumping (CNN, 10:16 p.m.). Reports were circulated about crisis reactions in other parts of the nation, e.g., reports that some people bought stocks of food, that gasoline prices had increased in some parts of the country, and that relatives who had been waiting in Los Angeles for passengers on the hijacked airplanes were offered grief counseling.

The debate about U.S. intelligence, bin Laden, retaliation, and international cooperation against terrorism continued among senators, former government officials, and experts, but no new statements were presented from the president, national leaders, or international leaders. Americans were trying to understand the mindset of the terrorists and how to defend themselves, and late in the evening, experts analyzed the events of the day from an historical perspective, among other things, talking about a fragmented world and about the power of symbols.

Stage Four: International

This period was characterized by the fact that it was past midnight on the East Coast of the United States. The president and most government officials were sleeping, while it was daytime in Europe and Asia. Most *news* came from international sources. While the viewers did not hear much from the world outside the United States during the previous stages, this period featured many international leaders who expressed support. CNN's Tom Fenton, vice president and deputy managing editor for international newsgathering, said in an interview with the author that several foreign heads of state contacted CNN and asked to have a statement broadcast because they wanted to distance their countries from the terrorism.

This period featured intense comments from around the world: Taliban Ambassador to Pakistan Abdul Salam Zaeef, Israeli Prime Minister Ariel Sharon, Palestine leader Chairman Yasir Arafat, British Prime Minister Tony Blair, Russian President Vladimir Putin, French President Jacques Chirac, German Chancellor Gerhard Schroeder, NATO Secretary-General George Robertson, and European Union President Guy Verhofstadt. Each had 10-50 seconds to express support for the United States (CNN,12:29 – 12:41 a.m.). More international comments followed later in the night.

In the hours to come, CNN also covered the international stock exchanges, told its viewers about the content of newspapers published elsewhere in the world and used experts based in Europe to discuss such issues as terrorism, bin Laden and the Palestinians' celebration in the streets (CNN, 1:37; 3:38; 4:22 a.m.). CNN broadcast live reports from Afghanistan (CNN, 2:32; 3:28; 4:18 a.m.) and Jerusalem, including an interview with Palestine Chairman Yasir Arafat, about the celebrating Palestinians (CNN, 2:42 a.m.).

The network also broadcast news from Germany, France, and Brussels that reflected concern about the role of United States in the world after 9/11. It was stated that many international companies had offices in the World Trade Center, and the American Red Cross had received international support from sister organizations. Secretary of State Colin Powell returned from an official trip to Peru and provided a statement in which he said enemies could neither destroy the American society nor its democracy.

Even though most of the *news* came from abroad, most *stories* were from the U.S. They consisted of three elements: (1) replay of footage shown during the day, (2) footage such as amatory video and longer on-the-street interviews that had been shot but not broadcast during the day, and (3) night reports from the WTC site, from traffic points in the city and from hospitals, where victims were treated, including reports about blood donations, the need for food and places to sleep for the rescue workers, and counseling for the victims. The pace was slower on these nightly reports and, along with more traditional news pieces, CNN also showed more narrative reports presented with a soft, sensitive tone that matched the hours (for example, CNN, 5:04 a.m.).

Behind the scene, political communicators and public relations personnel were at work. CNN reported that government officials during the night had briefings with journalists, telling them what the leaders intended to do the following day. Other communicators started spinning for special interests such as the need for economic stimuli and concerns about the economy of insurance companies. In the middle of the night, Gallup published the results of the first surveys done on 9/11, showing that 78 percent of the Americans were confident that President Bush would be able to handle the situation (CNN, 1:52 a.m.).

At the end of this period, the viewers were told that the light had been turned on in the White House indicating a new day had started (CNN, 5:46). The expression "911 national emergency" was introduced on CNN.

Stage Five: Mourning Begins

A new day had started. CNN focused on what people could expect to happen that day and in the days to come, and viewers were informed about their leaders' visions, goals, and strategies. This was a marked difference from the day before when no one knew what to expect next. Anchor Aaron Brown explained another difference between this day and the day before. He said:

> There was something sickeningly surreal about yesterday. At one point turning around, you watched these buildings collapse and you say that can't possibly be. If yesterday was surreal, today is about reality.... We are going to start to get a sense of how many people perished.... This will no longer be about buildings that collapsed. It's going to be about lives that have been shattered, families that have been shattered. It all feels to me quite different. (CNN, 7:50 a.m.)

On September 11, the catastrophe had swept over the East Coast. On September 12, it was possible to start estimating the damage. Now the rescue work at the World Trade Center could be seen in daylight on CNN. Only nine people had been rescued during the night, while many bodies were shipped away from the site, and hospitals were frustrated by the fact that they had received so few survivors. Hope continued for more survivors at The World Trade Center site, but no hope remained at the Pentagon. The names of flight crews and passengers on the four hijacked airplanes ran over the screen together with the names of four fire fighters who were known to be dead.

A period of mourning had started.

Focus was now again on U.S. internal affairs, but Colin Powell was surrounded by small flags from the whole world when he was interviewed about the need for international cooperation (CNN, 7:52 a.m.), and CNN presented interviews with Palestinian spokeswoman Hanna Ashrawi and Israeli former Prime Minister Ehud Barak—both of whom commented on the footage of Palestinians celebrating in the street the day before.

Sources and Journalistic Roles

The terrorist attacks were staged events that monopolized the media agenda on September 11, but the influence on the coverage of that agenda changed through the five stages.[17]

During the first stage, journalists saw it as their primary task to inform the American public and the rest of the world about what happened and to find sources who could provide interpretation. They used their instinct, knowledge, experience, and ethics to provide the public with relevant news.[18]

Three classical journalistic roles dominated this stage: the *news reporter*, the *watchdog* and the *interviewer as coordinator of a public debate*. The news reporters described what happened, the watchdogs asked critical questions concerning the CIA and FBI, and the interviewers organized a public debate that had long-lasting influence on world politics. FBI and CIA officials tried to influence public debate in response to accusations that they could have prevented the terrorist attacks. But, compared to later stages, the spin-doctors and political communicators had little to say during the first stage.

Eyewitness played an important role in the first stage in which viewers were desperate to hear what happened, and more than twenty individuals[19] shared their perception of what had happened at the disaster areas. Another major group of sources giving statements and interviews during this first stage was comprised of "former" government officials. In fact, seventeen former government officials shared their insights on terrorism and their opinions about what needed to be done, and some of them were interviewed more than once during the first ten hours. Compared to that, only thirteen members of the present political leadership, including members of Congress, President George W. Bush, New York Mayor Rudy Giuliani, New York Governor George Pataki, and some spokespersons gave interviews or public statements during this period. Statements also were presented from four international leaders, three representatives of the rescue work, and eight others.

It is notable that *former* government officials played a major role during the first stage in which one would expect eyewitnesses and present leaders to dominate. The former leaders interpreted the events, although, according to the stages suggested by scholars such as Graber and Schramm, these interpretations would first have been expected to play an important role later when the rescue work was well under way. At CNN, the Booking Department was responsible for finding and pre-interviewing interviewees, and on September 11, 2001, CNN had approximately 50,000 profiles in its database. Why did the staff choose to interview so many former officials?

Joy E. DiBenedetto, vice president for network bookings: "You know, you'll try for current, but most of the time current won't talk to you. And if they do it's like five minutes. It's not the kind of guest that you need to come on and be flexible and spend some time with you."

Cory Charles, director of international guest bookings: "You know you're sort of like first, second, third, fourth. You can go down the list until you get, hopefully, you get somebody up here."

When looking at the list of interviewees and public statements, it also is striking that they are primarily established, consensus-seeking politicians, diplomats, and former government officials. Journalists in the Booking Department explained:

Joy DiBenedetto: "Everybody's so responsive in times of crisis - like the chairman comes in … we don't want to put somebody on the air that says something that's premature or that somebody that doesn't have all the facts, and we're vetting people very closely, and in a time like 9/11, we did discuss who's the right person to put on."

Gail Chalef, managing editor of CNN network bookings: "In breaking news like that, the inclination is to speculate. And we like to stay as far away from speculating and just deliver, I mean I heard that over and over again in the first few days.… Well you were asking if we would book somebody who's angry at Muslims, well that's not balanced; that's not what we do."

The second stage was very different from the first. National political leaders and government officials now communicated their unity, leadership, and control of government, and they received full attention from CNN. Eighteen members of the present political leadership and government gave public statements or interviews, while seven "former" government officials participated. The only other interviewed source was a cardinal. No eyewitnesses, relatives of victims, or rescue workers from the disaster areas, no terrorism experts or airline officials had a word to say during the early primetime. This stage was dominated by highly professional political communicators.

In theory, CNN could have chosen not to broadcast the speech of the president or briefings by government officials, but in the historical context that was not a real choice. During the second stage, CNN primarily mediated the messages from the national government.

In the third stage, officials in charge of the rescue work used CNN as a channel for information to the public. This communication was provided by New York Mayor Rudy Giuliani, two police commissioners, a fire commissioner and a medical doctor. Fourteen eyewitnesses and relatives of victims provided the personal stories that allowed for identification. While parts of the coverage during this period consisted of transmissions from government and staged events like press briefings, this stage also contained journalistic news reports and public debates organized by CNN. Participating in these debates were six representatives of the present political leadership, five "former" government officials, and four other intellectuals.

In the fourth stage, most of the national political communicators left the spotlights, and CNN presented news from around the globe with time to *explore* areas little known to the general public. Among the sources interviewed or giving statements were eleven international leaders and experts compared to a total number of only nine American experts and political leaders.

Some journalists used these nightly hours for longer and more narrative formats than those known from breaking news stories, thereby introducing another classical journalistic role, the *narrator*, in the September 11 coverage. Among sources related to the scene of disaster were thirteen eyewitnesses and relatives of victims and four people involved in rescue work.

The fifth stage marked a new day, and its format clearly was reminiscent of the news format known in more normal days. Some journalists at CNN were briefed by government officials about upcoming events, while others reported from the rescue scene. Among the sources were nine people involved in the rescue work and six eyewitnesses/relatives. Also giving interviews were two recent government officials, three former and two international leaders.

While CNN during those first 24 hours exercised the classical journalistic roles—news hunter, watchdog, narrator, explorer, and chair of public debate—it also played an important role in managing the national crisis. A certain format exists for the coverage of national crisis, and some of the norms connected to that format will be further outlined in the chapter "Journalistic Norms: The Media as Shepherd."

Notes

1. WestGroup Research (2001, September 13). Americans Believe Attack on America TV Coverage Accurate; Anchors Professional, Press Release. Retrieved August 22, 2007, from *http://www.westgroupresearch.com/crisiscoverage/*; Pew Research Center for the People & the Press (September 19, 2001). American Psyche Reeling From Terror Attacks, Press Release. Retrieved August 22, 2007, from *http://people-press.org/reports/display.php3?ReportID=3*.
2. Pew Research Center for the People & the Press (September 19, 2001). *American Psyche Reeling From Terror Attacks*; Greenberg, B. S., Hofshire, L. & Lachlan, K. (2002). "Diffusion, Media Use and Interpersonal Communication Behaviors," In B.S. Greenberg (Ed.): *Communication and Terrorism: Public and Media Responses to 9/11* (pp. 3 – 216), Cresskill, NJ: Hampton Press.
3. Project for Excellence in Journalism with Princeton Survey Research Associates (January 28, 2002). Return to Normalcy? How the Media Have Covered the War on Terrorism, Press Release. Retrieved August 22, 2007, from http://www.journal-ism.org/node/281; WestGroup Research (September 13, 2001). Americans Believe Attack on America TV Coverage Accurate, Anchors Professional.
4. Zelizer, B. & Allan, S. (2002). Introduction: When Trauma Shapes the News, In B. Zelizer & S. Allan (Eds.): *Journalism after September 11,* (pp.1-24), New York: Routledge; Kellner, D. (2006). "September 11, Social Theory, and Democratic Politics," in A. P. Kavoori & T. Fraley (Eds.): *Media, terrorism, and theory* (pp. 161-178), Oxford: Rowman & Littlefield Publishers; Elliott, D. (2004). *Terrorism, Global Journalism, and the Myth of the Nation State, Journal of Mass Media Ethics,* 19(1), (pp. 29-45).
5. Mogensen, K. (2007). "How U.S. TV Journalists Talk About Objectivity in 9/11 Coverage," In T. Pludowski (Ed.): *How the World's News Media Reacted to 9/11: Essays from around the Globe* (pp. 301-318), Spokane, WA: Marquette Books LLC.
6. Neal, A. G. (1998). *National Trauma & Collective Memory: Major Events in the American Century* (pp. 9-12), New York: M. E. Sharpe Inc.
7. Schramm, W. (1965). "Communication in Crisis," In B.S. Greenberg & E. B. Parker (Eds.): *The Kennedy Assassination and the American Public: Social Communication in Crises* (pp.1-25), Stanford, CA: Stanford University Press; Neal, A. G. (1998). *National Trauma & Collective Memory: Major Events in the American Century* (pp. 9-12), New York: M. E. Sharpe Inc.; Lowrey, W. (2004). "Media Dependency During a Large-Scale Social Disruption: The Case of September 11," *Mass Communication and Society*, Vol. 7 (3), (pp. 339-357).
8. Neal, A. G. (1998). *National Trauma & Collective Memory: Major Events in the American Century*, New York: M. E. Sharpe Inc.
9. Mindak, W. H. & Hursh, G. D. (1965). "Television's Function on the Assassination Weekend," In B.S. Greenberg & E. B. Parker (Eds.): *The Kennedy Assassination and the American Public: Social Communication in Crises* (pp. 130-141), Stanford, CA: Stanford University Press; OECD (2003) Emerging Systemic Risks in the 21st Century: An Agenda for Action, OECD's International Futures Programme. Retrieved July 27, 2006, from *http://www.unisdr.org/eng/library/Literature/7754.pdf.*
10. Schramm, W. (1965). "Communication in Crisis," in B.S. Greenberg & E. B. Parker (Eds.): *The Kennedy Assassination and the American Public: Social Communication in Crises* (pp.1-25), Stanford, CA: Stanford University Press.
11. Graber, D. A. (1980). *Mass Media and American Politics*. Washington DC: Congressional Quarterly Press.
12. This last paragraph is copied from Mogensen, K., Lindsay, L., Li, X., Perkins, J.,

& Beardsley, M. (2002). "How TV News Covered the Crisis: The Content of CNN, CBS, ABC, NBC and Fox," in B.S. Greenberg (Ed.): *Communication and Terrorism: Public and Media Responses to 9/11* (pp. 101 – 120), Cresskill, NJ: Hampton Press.

13. Schramm, W. (1965). Communication in Crisis; Graber, D. A. (1980). *Mass Media and American Politics.*

14. The following table is also printed in Mogensen, K. (2007). "How U.S. TV Journalists Talk About Objectivity in 9/11 Coverage," in T. Pludowski (Ed.): *How the World's News Media Reacted to 9/11: Essays from around the Globe* (pp. 301-318), Spokane, WA: Marquette Books LLC.

15. Mogensen, K., Lindsay, L., Li, X., Perkins, J., & Beardsley, M. (2002). "How TV News Covered the Crisis: The Content of CNN, CBS, ABC, NBC and Fox," in B.S. Greenberg (Ed.): *Communication and Terrorism: Public and Media Responses to 9/11* (pp. 101 – 120), Cresskill, NJ: Hampton Press.

16. Mogensen, K. (2007). "How U.S. TV Journalists Talk About Objectivity in 9/11 Coverage," in T. Pludowski (Ed.): *How the World's News Media Reacted to 9/11: Essays from around the Globe* (pp. 301-318), Spokane, WA: Marquette Books LLC.

17. This paragraph and some parts of the following text have previously been published in Mogensen, K (2007). How U.S. TV Journalists Talk About Objectivity in 9/11 Coverage.

18. Mogensen, K., Lindsay, L., Li, X., Perkins, J., & Beardsley, M. (2002). "How TV News Covered the Crisis: The Content of CNN, CBS, ABC, NBC and Fox."

19. The numbers of eyewitnesses and relatives of victims shown on CNN are estimated on the basis of videotapes provided by Vanderbilt University. In some cases it was not possible to identify sources. Replays are eliminated from the numbers if identified.

3

Cruising on Autopilot:
How the Media Covered 9/11

Jay Perkins and Xigen Li

Covering a national disaster is a bit like swallowing a live oyster. If you think about it too much, it probably won't get done.

That was the situation facing television crews and executives on 9/11, and that was the way they approached the task. Executive after executive and reporter after reporter all sang the same refrain: "We didn't plan our coverage. We reacted to the situation. We didn't have time to think about it. We survived on our instincts, our training and our experience. We did it by rote."

That might sound strange to anyone not familiar with the way the media work. After all, no disaster like 9/11 had ever occurred. So how could it be done by rote? Nevertheless, the comments of reporters and research into the story-selection process both supported that conclusion.

Academic research shows that when the social order is seriously disrupted, people usually desire more information than the media can provide.[1] During a crisis, the public becomes dependent on the media for news that may be vital for survival and for important messages from public and private authorities. They look to the media for information, explanations, and interpretations.[2]

This need for media information and explanation becomes greater as the crisis grows larger. For example, the Kennedy assassination resulted in greater need for interpretation, explanation, and consolation.[3] The public wanted desperately to understand what it meant.

A note on academic research is in order here. Research on media operations tends to concentrate on the types of stories produced (the content) and the context in which those stories are presented (the frame). Media frame includes content but also considers emphasis, elaboration, and exclusion. One researcher described framing as the "story angle or hook, the central organizing idea or story line that provides meaning to an unfolding strip of events and weaves a connection among them."[4]

The theory behind media framing is that the media not only set an agenda with story presentation but also transfer specific values to issues by the way they present the story. The concept has its critics, most of who argue that the lack of precise definitions makes media framing suspect. Nevertheless, it generally is accepted, and a large body of research has been done using the technique.

This study seeks to determine whether story selection (the type of stories produced) and coverage framing are dependent on the time of coverage. Previous studies and common sense indicate that coverage frames will be affected by time, particularly in a crisis when media and governmental resources are strained to handle the immediate circumstance.

Common sense was vindicated. This content analysis found that stage of crisis was an important factor in determining coverage framing.

It also was determined that a dynamic model, rather than the static models used in most media research, should be considered when analyzing framing during a lengthy crisis such as 9/11. Media coverage, unsurprisingly, focuses on different key issues at different stages of the event.

This study examined the first twenty-four hours of television network coverage of the attacks on the World Trade Center and the Pentagon on September 11, 2001. Television networks were chosen because television has been the dominant medium in informing the American people about the terrorist attacks and the war on terrorism that followed.[5] The news coverage of five networks (ABC, CBS, NBC, CNN, and FOX News) was selected for content analysis because of their dominant status in television news coverage in the United States.

News content of the five television networks was acquired through Vanderbilt University's video library. A total of 2,647 stories was identified from the 24 hours of coverage, including 745 stories from ABC, 612 stories from CBS, 427 from NBC, 657 from CNN, and 206 for FOX News.

The formal study itself was expanded through interviews of many of the journalists who made the decisions on that day. These included reporters and editors at the three broadcast networks (ABC, CBS and

NBC) and the three major cable news networks (CNN, FOX, and MS-NBC), resulting in more than a thousand pages of transcript.

Interviews with those who actually made the decisions provided an interesting counterpoint to the academic research. The professionals tended not to think in terms of the type of story produced. Instead, their discussions were centered on specific decisions that had to be made to cover the event, that is, what personnel to move to which locations, which reporters to assign which task, which studio personnel to assign which time slots. Little thought appears to have been given to the percentage of time coverage that was focused on the disaster versus coverage of safety issues versus coverage of impact on the environment.

Breaking News Requires Experience, Instinct

In short, while academics tend to view the news product as something that results from conscious decision-making (and thus something that can be, with analysis, a window into real-time journalistic thinking), the professionals tend to think of the product as something that happens because they follow basic rules of journalism, their "gut instinct," and their past experiences. Bill Felling, national editor at CBS News, summed up this professional thinking that too much can be made of story selection and placement when he said "crisis management is done by rote. If you had to think at the moment of crisis, you couldn't do anything. You just have to do it by instinct."

Often, this instinct is supplemented by taking advantage of what happens to be available. "In breaking coverage … you put almost anything on as soon as you get it," said Steve Friedman, senior executive producer for *The Early Show* on CBS. "You put them (the reporters) on and hope for the best. By the second day, you return to the editorial function of seeing it before you put it on. The first day is more like a war where you have to mass your troops ... get your Washington people up, get your people all around the country to report on what the effect is there, people overseas," he said. "You go with your instinct and what you have been taught over the years. You live and die by what you do."

Those instincts went into effect immediately when word of the first plane crash into the World Trade Center was relayed to the CNN headquarters in Atlanta. Paul Varien, managing editor of CNN newswires, said he and other managers had just sat down for the first planning session of the day. The plane crash was not discussed, however. Instead, "everybody immediately got up out of their chairs and ran down to the newsroom" to begin working on disaster coverage.

Camera crews and reporters had to be assigned to cover the disaster itself in the early hours, and executives often found themselves scrambling to fly or drive in reporters and cameras from outside New York and Washington. The massive focus needed on the disaster itself in the early hours left few resources available for covering peripheral or broad explanatory issues. The availability of personnel changed during the day as more reporters and more cameras could be brought to bear on the story.

This personnel problem was graphically illustrated in a series of interviews with CBS personnel. The first plane, American Airlines Flight 11, hit the North Tower of the World Trade Center at 8:46 a.m., during *The Early Show* on CBS. Most of the people who produce the *CBS Evening News* were not even at work. So the first consideration for CBS News was how to stay on top of the story with limited personnel, how to get in touch with the personnel it needed to cover the story and how to assign them to the right locations.

Marcy McGinnis, senior vice president of CBS News, was an early arrival. She planned to stop by the office early that day because she was on her way to Nashville. She got word of the first crash when a friend in New Jersey called her to tell her that the World Trade Center was on fire.

"I was in a cab literally two blocks from here (CBS News), and so I ran to the newsroom. We called (*The Early Show* personnel) and said 'stay on the air' until we can get Dan Rather in here and get the control room up. Our control room people weren't in yet because they don't normally come in that early," McGinnis said.

While CBS struggled to cover the story with the personnel already on duty, the news staff was being quickly alerted.

"My deputy (national editor Bill Felling) is already sending camera crews, producers, correspondents, satellite trucks; he is doing all of that stuff. So I go in there and say 'what have you done. Who is on their way? What else can we do?' And meanwhile we are trying to get everybody and their brother in to work, knowing that this is going to be big enough that we are going to have to stay on," McGinnis said.

Coverage Changes as the News Event Unfolds

Under these circumstances, it is not surprising, that coverage frames changed during the different stages of crisis. The study also suggested stage of crisis had some effect on media function in a crisis and that media inform, explain and interpret the news event as it unfolds.

During the first stage, from 8:45 a.m. to 11 a.m., coverage was framed primarily as stories about the disaster (56.8 percent). Other stories were framed as political (14.8 percent), criminal and terrorism (12.5 percent) and safety concerns (8.9 percent). During the second stage, from 11 a.m. to 3 p.m., the coverage framed as a disaster (37.8 percent) declined dramatically. Political frames increased during the early stages of the coverage, rising from 14.8 percent at 11 a.m. to 28.5 percent at 3 p.m.

The economy frame began to emerge in the later hours of this stage. Economic stories started at 0.9 percent in the first stage and averaged 1.9 percent during this second stage. Safety frame stories increased significantly from 8.9 percent in the first stage to 11.3 percent in the second stage before topping out at 19 percent the next morning. Criminal and terrorism frames dropped from 12.5 percent to 11.6 percent during the second stage, just slightly below its average for the 24-hour period.

Coverage after 7 p.m. presented a different pattern. Stories with a political frame decreased from their high of 28.5 percent during the second stage to 17 percent during this fourth stage (7 p.m. to midnight) and only 12.6 percent in the fifth stage (midnight to 6 a.m.). Economics became an evident frame, moving from its low of 0.9 percent in the first stage to its high of 4.1 percent. Human safety became the second most dominant frame in the period after midnight, rising to its high of 19 percent in the 6 a.m. to 9 a.m. time slot. Human interest frames also showed a significant increase after midnight in the time allotted to coverage.

In addition, differences did exist in coverage frames among the networks. Four major coverage frames were identified. The three network stations—ABC, CBS, and NBC—had fewer stories framed as political than the cable stations. CBS had the most stories with a criminal frame, and NBC had the fewest. ABC, CNN, and FOX News had a similar number of stories framed as criminal and terrorism.

The networks devoted more attention to the safety frame than did CNN and FOX. While stories with human interest frames did not gain much space from the networks, ABC (7.5 percent) and CBS (7.8 percent) had more stories with the human interest frame than other networks. FOX deviated from other networks in coverage frames, providing more political frames than other networks but few stories framed as safety and human interest. CNN was close to FOX in several coverage frames.

These results also confirmed the hypothesis advanced by Doris Graber in 1980 and the National Research Council Committee on Disasters and the Mass Media in that the functions of television news go through distinct stages during a crisis.

The council postulated that the press had the following functions during a crisis: (1) warning of predicted or impending disasters; (2) conveying information to officials, relief agencies, and the public; (3) charting the progress of relief and recovery; (4) dramatizing lessons learned for purpose of future preparedness; (5) taking part in long-term public education programs; and (6) defining slow-onset problems as crises or disasters.[6]

Graber, by comparison, divided the stages into thirds. During her first stage, media are the prime sources not only for the general public but also for public officials concerned with the crisis. Journalists' key roles are to describe what has happened and to help coordinate the relief work. Their top priority is to get accurate information, which, even if it is bad news, relieves uncertainty and calms people.[7] In the second stage, media coverage of events focuses on making sense out of the situation. Plans are formulated and implemented to address the needs of the victims and to repair the damage. Graber suggested that the third stage overlaps the first two. In an effort to provide context, the role of media is to place the crisis in a larger, longer-term perspective.

This study divided the twenty-four hours into six different stages. The first two stages are identical to Graber's first two stages. The last four stages in this study overlap her third stage.

During the first stage of 9/11, disaster stories dominated, while stories with political and criminal frames were still evolving. As the coverage proceeded into the second stage, the disaster frame declined, and political and criminal frames increased. During the third stage, stories framed as human interest increased slightly, and issues concerning the environment and economy began to surface. The findings suggest when an event goes through rapid development, the media coverage frames are likely to follow with a series of frames dominant in turn at different stages.

The findings on effect of stages of crisis have important implications in frame analysis of media content. While most analysis deals with issues not under rapid changes, a dynamic view of frame changes over time allows frame analysis to reflect the coverage more accurately. Coverage frames usually do not remain constant.

Story Focus Changes in Different Crisis Stages

This study also sought to determine whether story selection was dynamic and thus the types of stories shown would change during the different stages of crisis. This was determined to be true.

During the first stage, from 8:45 a.m. to 11 a.m., the key issues identified were description of the incident (30.6 percent), severity of disaster (17.9 percent), terrorism (15.6 percent), safety concerns (12.9 percent), and U.S. government reaction (10 percent). During the second stage of the coverage, from 11 a.m. to 3 p.m., descriptions of the incident declined dramatically (11.3 percent) while severity of disaster (18.5 percent) and safety concerns (11.3 percent) remained the same. The issue of terrorism increased somewhat (17.1 percent), while U.S. government reaction (17.5 percent) and rescue efforts (10.1 percent) increased significantly. After 3 p.m., descriptions of the disaster decreased significantly and were no longer a dominant issue.

Instead, rescue effort arose as an issue. However, severity of disaster (15.6 percent) remained high, and safety concerns (12.8 percent) increased. Victims of tragedy (4.9 percent) and economic impact (4.3 percent) also became more prominent as issues as the coverage moved to the later stages.

These results reconfirm the importance of the stage in understanding media coverage of a crisis. It is consistent with the notion advanced by previous studies that themes and issues covered by the media change over time. Media quickly shift from presenting the terrifying effects to a strategy of "othering."[8]

This study demonstrated when the shift took place in the coverage of a crisis of this magnitude and to what degree the changes occurred from one stage to another. Key issues were closely related to coverage frames. The findings also suggest that coverage of a major crisis is a dynamic process involving evident changes of frames and key issues as the events related to the crisis unfold.

That the nature of what is covered during a disaster constantly shifts is not news to the media professionals. It simply is a logical progression as reporters and editors throw their effort into first covering the immediate. If they are not in a position to cover the immediate—for example, if they are working in a city where the disaster did not occur—they cover what they can cover locally. Once the immediate needs are met, reporters move to reaction stories and to analytical stories. In other words, to use their parlance, who and what gets covered first; why and how has to wait.

That said, it was not surprising that the editors and reporters interviewed didn't attach much significance to the way the story unfolded or when event coverage shifted. The decision of when to shift from one frame to another wasn't intellectual, they said, nor was it the result of following a manual for disaster coverage. It was simply the product of past experience.

"It was instinct," said Al Ortiz, of CBS. "It was thinking, you know, well 'we haven't talked about the Pentagon in a long time. Let's talk about the Pentagon now.'—that kind of thing."

Robert Denbo, head of the national news assignment desk at NBC News, said it well: "We knew what to do, and we did it and we didn't think (about it)," he said. Steve Friedman, senior executive producer for *The Early Show* at CBS, agreed that training and instincts were the keys to handling a situation such as 9/11. "I don't think that in a situation like that you study manuals. I think you go with your instinct and what you have been taught over the years."

And Jim Murphy, executive producer of CBS News, said it is really a matter of having people "with a lot of experience and good decision-making ability being in the right place at the right time."

Advance Planning Gives Direction but Few Specifics

As for planning, little existed, and the planning didn't really deal with what issues would be covered. Instead, the planning dealt with how resources would be marshaled.

McGinnis of CBS noted a second decision that had to be made at CBS was when to transfer control of the coverage from the *Early Show*, which ended at 10 a.m., to Dan Rather and the regular news team.

"You know one of the big ones was—and in the scheme of things it was not a huge decision—but it was 'when do we go over from the (Bryant) Gumbel gang, from the *Early Show* gang, over to Dan Rather?' Dan got in the building pretty quickly, but then the decision was 'when can we actually put him in the chair and go with him?' because we didn't have enough of the control room staff to do that. So there was a lot of discussion (about) should we wait until after 10 a.m., should we try to go on earlier, which could be a disaster because what you don't want is to have Dan in the chair and have nothing to say."

Al Ortiz, director of special events for CBS, gave another example of the types of decisions the news crew had to make.

"There are a lot of fast decisions you have to make, such as 'IS there something on a particular camera,' 'Do you want to go to this other camera?' There is footage coming into the building, and (you're) trying to identify what it is and what you are seeing. What I had to do was delegate enough responsibility to the people around me so they could come to me with a recommendation of what to show next, or where to go next, or who was going to have a news conference next."

The result of this pressure, said CBS's Murphy, was that many decisions were made on the spot in casual meetings.

"We and a couple of other people, just sort of in an ad hoc manner, ran into each other in the newsroom and said 'OK, you know we got to figure out exactly how we are going to do this.' We decided how to divide up the day and split the news division into units so it would be the daytime unit that's working with special events, and the morning people doing the morning thing.

"We (CBS *Evening News*) would handle several hours in the evening and then the *Primetime* people would do an hour special that gets expanded, repeated, changed around as it goes across the country from 10 p.m. until 1 or 2 in the morning and then up-to-the-minute time. So we figured that out quickly. Everybody knows very well how to run their own unit, plus everybody involved has done a lot of live television."

Finding Sources

Prior research shows the media tend to focus on governmental sources in a crisis situation involving national interest. That was certainly true on 9/11. Government officials were the dominant sources used in the coverage with witnesses running a distant second. However, the use of governmental sources was less than that found in other disaster stories, indicating the possibility of limits to the ability of government to control or even to respond to news requirements in a disaster.

About 19.3 percent of the stories used government officials as sources, while 10.8 percent of the stories quoted witnesses. When government officials were used as sources, the stories addressed issues regarding government reaction and policies. Key issues associated with government sources included terrorism, government reaction, rescue efforts, and safety concerns. When witnesses were quoted, the stories focused mostly on what happened at the World Trade Center and the Pentagon. Key issues associated with witnesses were recounting the incident and the severity of disaster.

While government officials were among the major sources in the overall coverage, they were not overwhelmingly dominant as in the coverage of a continuing and widespread crisis involving national interest. Source use became more diversified in the later stages of the coverage.

Several possible reasons may help explain the less-than-expected use of governmental sources. One is that government officials were caught as flatfooted as everyone else on 9/11. Accurate information was difficult to come by in the first hours because no one knew what was happening.

"An interesting thing on that day, nobody knew," said Brian Kennedy, National Desk, ABC News. "I mean a lot of people we talked to on the phone, officials, they didn't know what was going on. And they tried to tell you as best as they could. One of the things ... I remember from that day was that people would tell you things, and they were just flat wrong."

The Media as Backchannel for Government

When the situation is so confused that even government does not know what is happening, the media become not just conveyers of information to the general public but intelligence backchannels for governmental officials.

This use of the media as intelligence backchannels was seen clearly in the first war with Iraq when CNN's television crew embedded in Baghdad was broadcasting live as the cruise missiles hit the city. CNN not only was showing the public what was happening in Baghdad. It was showing military planners and government leaders how well the targets had been hit, how well the missiles had performed, how the Iraqi government was responding.

Clearly, some of that was going on in the initial hours of 9/11. Television had live cameras on the scene in New York. The pictures and commentary were important sources of information for government leaders in Washington. The cameras provided access to information agents in the field could not provide—and the cameras did so dispassionately, without the filters of human intelligence.

Paul Salvin, executive producer for *ABC World News Tonight*, said he believed media were backchannels for government, especially in those first few hours.

"I think they were relying on the networks for information, not just the networks, everybody. They rely on cable and everyone," Salvin said. "That's not that unusual. Very often the government is relying on our information for things, as they should. You know why? We're good information gatherers."

A second reason governmental sources were not as prevalent as normal might well have been the lack of access. Much of the government was in hiding for the first few hours. The president, for example, was shuttled from air base to air base aboard Air Force One. The Capitol complex was deserted as members of Congress stayed away from a potential target. Those members of the administrative and legislative branches who could be located often were in briefings or held in secure areas.

Al Ortiz, executive producer, Special Events for CBS, said this caused even more reliance on witnesses and the observations made by reporters on the scene. "You know, there weren't a lot of officials to go to at that point."

Lester Holt, anchor for MSNBC, agreed.

"I think we wanted to rely on them at least to confirm or to dispel things like the (car) bomb (report) at the State Department. It was very hard to get the government's indication on that."

Reporters also had already learned that the Bush administration was not as user-friendly with reporters as some previous administrations. As a consequence, they looked to other sources of information quickly rather than wait for comment from a governmental source who they expected to stonewall them.

"I think the Bush administration has basically done a pretty good job of controlling, I don't know if controlling the coverage, but setting the boundaries," said Paul Varien, managing editor of *CNN Newswires*.

Matt Lauer, host of the *NBC Today Show*, agreed.

> This is not an administration that has been overly open any way with us. It is a little different. It has been different from day one.... I think (Secretary of Defense Donald) Rumsfeld set the tone pretty early on when questions would come up at the Pentagon, he would basically respond "Are you kidding me? You really think I am going to answer that? Yes I know that, but I am not going to tell you." And I think that was pretty much a sharp signal to all of us as to what would and would not be discussed.

The clampdown on information was not just at the federal level. Robert Dembo of NBC News noted that New York officials also were difficult to quote.

> Information was parceled out under a very controlled circumstance by the mayor of the city of New York and by emergency officials. And to this day we can't really know what was withheld from us. I think under the guise of security, the press was needlessly kept away from the focus of the story. But I am not suggesting that there was any kind of organized disinformation campaign or (an attempt to) limit information campaign. I just think that the people in charge had to balance security and our right of access.

Technology Reduces Need for Government Sources

Other factors were at work, of course, in the limitation on the use of governmental sources.

For one, technology and databases have made it possible for reporters to get corroborating evidence without having to talk to a governmental source directly. Flight information may be obtained from airline websites, for example. Maintenance records may be obtained over the Internet from the FAA's database in Oklahoma City. Seating capacity, types of engines, and other technical data may be obtained from aircraft manufacturer websites. All this technology was put to good use on 9/11.

"Independently, my producer was pulling up flight information because, you know, I think we knew it was a Boston plane that was missing, got the flight number, from the airline website," said Lester Holt, anchor for MSNBC. "And I was able to say now, there is a flight whatever it was, that goes from Boston to Los Angeles. It would have left Boston at such and such a time and would be due in L.A. We believe that to be the airplane."

Another possible factor is that the scope of the disaster was so huge that the networks were strained to just keep up with the immediate needs of disaster coverage. Television requires massive behind-the-scenes resources (camera crews, film editors, production crews), and the networks never have had the reporting resources of the major newspapers. Washington reporters normally would have been focused on tracking down the government angles and government officials, but they had their own disaster to cover—the crash of American Airlines Flight 77 into the Pentagon complex. Additionally, the uncertainty of the first few hours and the number of airplanes still in the air meant the networks had to keep their resources under tight controls until they could decide what other targets might be hit.

And then, of course, the internal dynamics of journalism—the need to get corroborating information from diverse sources—were at work. This mitigates the amount of information tied to governmental representatives in all stories. It particularly mitigated it on 9/11, when the government itself did not seem to know much about what was happening.

"Our general rule, kind of the rule that everybody has for that matter— AP, any broadcaster, wire service, newspaper—you need two sources to say something," said Bill Felling, national editor for CBS News.

Robert Dembo, head of the national news assignment desk for NBC, agreed. "We did not suspend our sourcing (requirements.) The temptation when you have a story of this magnitude, unprecedented magnitude or at least not since the Second World War, is to just go with whatever comes in and report it. But at the same time, if used during the coverage of stories of this magnitude, you absolutely have to be right."

Jim Murphy, executive producer for *CBS Evening News*, agreed. "Everything gets checked. Depending on the kind of information it was and how important it was, some of it is a one-source thing, some is two, some is multiple. Some of it is like 'There is no way I am doing that unless somebody says on camera it is true; and that somebody is important.'"

This reliance on more than one source, the reluctance of government officials to confirm or deny some rumors, and the uncertainty of the reporters themselves about what was going on all contributed to the air of cautionary journalism on 9/11.

"I think any time you're involved in a breaking event, your ability to fact check, to source and the rest diminishes some. But it didn't diminish to the point where we were just putting out bald-faced rumor or any one's opinion. But everything was delivered, I think, with a lot of caveats, you know what we know and when we know it," said Paul Salvin, executive producer of ABC's *World News Tonight*.

And finally, the implications of the event on the international scene meant that foreign leaders wanted to be interviewed, and foreign policy implications had to be explored. This diluted the amount of time that might otherwise have been given to U.S. governmental sources.

"We had a lot of heads of state come to us wanting to be interviewed because that was the only way they could get their message to the United States," said Tom Fenton, vice president and deputy managing editor for international newsgathering at CNN. He noted that many foreign leaders feared a backlash against the Arab citizens in their countries as well as a backlash against Arab nations and wanted to use U.S. media to possibly defuse some of this backlash.

"People who are really hard to get suddenly were making themselves available," he said. Fenton said his department took as many incoming calls and video feeds as possible from foreign leaders and used them all.

Whatever the reason, the findings suggest a weakened role of government sources during the early stages of a crisis situation involving national interest. This finding is consistent with Brigitte Nacos' argument that media use different methods when covering an anti-American terrorist act than when covering other foreign policy issues.

Nacos analyzed the press' role in reporting terrorism (Iran hostage crisis 1979-81, TWA hijacking in 1985, hijacking of Achille Lauro in 1985). That research concluded that media, rather than relying on traditional administrative sources, called on a variety of sources, including terrorists and their allies, families of the victims, and critics of the establishment.[9] The findings indicate that the degree to which a variety of sources will be used in the coverage depends not only on the nature of the incident but also the focus of the coverage.

What Pictures Should Be Provided?

While reporters worried about finding good sources, producers had a different headache: how much information should be shown. Some of the pictures from the scene were visually gripping. But some also showed people dying.

Because of the pace required to cover the disaster, those decisions also were made immediately, sometimes after the pictures already had run. Each network made its own call. Ortiz, for example, said CBS showed the first shots of people jumping or falling from the World Trade Center inadvertently.

"Within about two or three hours, there was a lot of videotape coming into the building, both by courier and being fed in by trucks. We took some of those live as they were being fed in, and we didn't have time to review the tapes or take the time to review the tapes. And on several of those, you saw things like victims falling, and bodies identifiable and that sort of thing," he said.

"I consulted with the president of the news division who was in the control room with me, and we agreed if we showed that again it would be done moderately, and we would prepare the viewer for it by having Dan (Rather) warn them about what we were going to see. But as more information came in, we used those pictures less and less so I think we probably ran pictures the first time sight unseen when they came in and maybe once or twice with some warnings later in the day."

Murphy said CBS's decisions about what film to show were made all day.

"That went on all day the first day," he said. "A shot would run and then people would go 'uhhh' like that, and it is too much. Let's not use it again. We would talk about it or call our bosses. This was coming from all over the place. I mean it was a real huge team effort. Somebody could be watching across the street in another office (and they would call and say) you guys just aired a shot where I saw, yada yada, and people would go back and look at it and go like 'OK. Let's make sure that this does not get used again. Mark the tape.'

"Some of them were incredibly gruesome. You know all the people jumping out of the buildings and stuff like that. There is just no reason to, there is just no reason to give it to people over and over, there is just no reason."

The Role of Planning

Even though the news executives agreed that experience got them through the first twenty-four hours of coverage, that does not mean they had no advance planning. Several network executives pointed to action plans for covering disasters, and some said they even had plans drawn up for covering a terrorist attack on New York City. But they agreed the plans were something done in advance and as preparation and not something consulted and followed on the day of the event.

However, Brian Kennedy, ABC News desk, said the advance planning two years earlier was critical to the performance of his unit on 9/11.

We had meetings with the Office of Emergency Management about two years before this happened about a major terrorist attack in the city. This was based on the 1993 bombing and some other things that happened, the Embassy bombings. Right after that, we started saying okay this city's probably in a tough place. And we were lucky enough to meet with the OEM folks. But if you write anything when this happens, there's no chance to go back and read it. So hopefully, what you remember from writing it down is what you go on—and the fact that many people have been around, have been doing this for a long time.

Keith McAllister, senior vice president and national managing editor for *CNN* News in Atlanta, agreed advance planning and post mortems that assess how well something worked were essential ingredients in newsgathering.

"When I was the New York bureau chief and when I was deputy there, we went through several iterations of writing a manual for breaking news because as young people or new people come in, you want to train them. I mean you've got to have a plan. And to the extent that what you need to write it down, or the extent to which it needs to be discussed and all that, we continually do that.

"We have earthquake plans for L.A. and San Francisco that we've been revising annually for 20 years. We add equipment out there and there's also procedural things that we do all the time, like we always make sure that we have access to satellite trucks in places where we absolutely have to have them."

The news executives all said their plans of action of 9/11 worked fairly well, and few revisions would be needed for the future.

"We haven't gone back to the plan and made revisions," said ABC's Brian Kennedy. "We sort of have a new plan of our own which is not written down the way the first one was. But not much has changed. Some things have changed, some things that we were lucky on or some things that we weren't able to react to quickly, mostly technology stuff, communication."

He noted, however, that training was a continual exercise. "There's a lot of training with gas masks, fire hazard suits, that sort of thing is going on," he said. "There's always a greater sense that this could happen again. So everything you do, you have that in the back of your mind so you're ready and preparing every day for that, that story to happen again, I guess, unfortunately."

CNN's McAllister also said he had not made any significant revisions to the coverage plans as a result of 9/11. "Our breaking news plan worked actually very well. The thing that we weren't entirely prepared for, I don't think anybody was, was covering terrorism incidents in the United States."

McAllister noted, however, that 9/11 and other terrorist activity had changed the level of training given to his reporters and would change the way his reporters were taught to operate.

"We spent a huge amount of time bringing in experts and consultants to deal with the issue of 'how do you cover potential WMD incidents in the U.S.,'" he said. He mentioned the anthrax scares in which envelopes stuffed with the potentially deadly bacteria were sent through the U.S. mail to various people. "When the anthrax stuff started happening, we weren't flatfooted. We've had seminars here at the bureau chiefs meeting two years ago and we did a whole kind of seminars for people here."

McAllister noted that the government's first news conference after the anthrax scare was held in the Brentwood, N.J., postal facility. "And we learned shortly thereafter that everybody in that facility had been exposed because the stuff had been aerosolized and moved around the building....

"Our first instinct (has always been) to run inside and get close to the story," McAllister said. "Well, if you think it's a potentially a WMD incident, you don't do that. You stand outside. We've had to fundamentally address the question of how we approach newsgathering in a different way. We hadn't said (in the past) you're going to do it differently next time. And so now what we say to people is, 'If there's a potentially dangerous thing, don't go in the building, don't get the picture, don't worry about it, stand back.'"

Notes

1.   Neal, A. G. (1998). *National Trauma & Collective Memory: Major Events in the American Century.* New York: M. E. Sharpe Inc.

2. Graber, D. A. (1980). *Mass Media and American Politics*. Washington DC: Congressional Quarterly Press, Pg. 228.
3. Schramm, W. (1965). Communication in Crisis. In B. S. Greenberg & E. B. Parker (Eds.): *The Kennedy Assassination and the American Public: Social Communication in Crisis* (pp.1-25), Stanford, CA: Stanford University Press.
4. Gamson, W. & Modigliana, A. (1993). The changing culture of affirmative action, *Research in Political Sociology*, 3, 137-177.
5. Stempel, G., & Hargrove, T. (2002). Media Sources of Information and Attitudes about Terrorism. In B. S. Greenberg (Ed.): *Communication and Terrorism*, Creskill, NJ: Hampton Press.
6. National Research Council Committee on Disasters in the Mass Media (1979). *Disasters in the Mass Media: Proceedings of the Committee on Disasters and the Mass Media Workshop* (pp. 10). Washington, DC: National Academy Press.
7. Graber, D. A. (1980). *Mass Media and American Politics*.
8. Ungar, S. (1998, March). Hot crises and media reassurance: A comparison of emerging diseases and Ebola Zaire, *The British Journal of Sociology*, 49, (1), 36-56.
9. Nacos, B. (1994). *Terrorism and the Media: From the Iran Hostage Crisis to the Oklahoma City Bombing*. New York: Columbia University Press.

4

Consolation: Was It a Virtual Catharsis?

Xigen Li and Jay Perkins

It's been accepted doctrine for well over two decades that media bring people together, give them direction and provide a healing catharsis during a crisis.[1] The journalists in this study, perhaps aware of that expectation, nevertheless said their focus during the first twenty-four hours after the attacks on the World Trade Center in New York and the Pentagon in Washington, D.C., was not on providing reassurance. They were too busy trying to explain what happened.

And yet, the public seemed to gain such consolation. That happened as journalists focused on the need to be professional, to provide precise and accurate information, to tell viewers what could be confirmed and what could not and to avoid creating panic by going beyond what was known.

Perhaps that's the point. This analysis found that media concentrated almost totally on providing information and facts to the public. Specific stories that could be considered consoling or healing made up less than 5 percent of the total stories provided by television in the immediate aftermath of the attack—and that high came more than six hours after the first aircraft was steered into the World Trade Center.

"It's rarely ever our business to reassure the nation," said Bill Wheatly of NBC News. "Our business is to bring in the information. Now if that information is reassuring, that's the way it should be. But we really are in the news business. And I think it is almost always reassuring when you present people with information that keeps them up-to-the-minute as to what's going on."

Perhaps a caveat is in order here. Even though this research showed that consolation and guiding were not deliberate factors in the coverage, the tone of the coverage—the demeanor of the reporters, the seriousness of the voices, the inflections—clearly all played a role in calming the public. These are not factors that can be recorded by traditional content analysis, and yet they may be as significant as the words used or the stories selected.

People Appreciate Positive Tone on Television

Even if most journalists did not consciously focus on consolation, the tone of the coverage certainly was a positive factor among American citizens. Several journalists mentioned the large number of congratulatory letters and emails they received. Clearly, some in the audience found consolation and healing, even if it was more in the minds of that audience than in the reality of the coverage.

"We got an enormous amount of e-mail and letters and phone calls following the event that were very complimentary of the tone we maintained, which is surprising because there was no conscious effort," said Matt Lauer, co-anchor of NBC's *Today Show*.

"It wasn't that we were saying, 'OK, what tone do we want to strike here?.' But people were very impressed by the fact that we did not start (playing) Chicken Little (and acting like) it is the end of the world, even though we may have thought that way."

And, of course, many of the journalists were not unaware of the public's need for reassurance. Some said the tone they adopted on 9/11 came naturally without too much thought. Others did acknowledge they made conscious decisions about the tone of their coverage.

"It didn't need to be hyped with some of the usual games that go on in our business," said Steve Capus, executive director of NBC's *Nightly News*. "It didn't need a whole lot of adjectives thrown up against it. It didn't need cheesy promotional material attached to it."

Paul Salvin, executive producer of *ABC Nightly News*, added: "Imagine if you turned on the set, and the anchorman burst into tears and he's running around. You know, there is a calming quality just in the mere fact that somebody is telling you something, and that's what we were there to do. We were to tell them what it was that we knew, as accurately as possible under very trying circumstances, at a time when everybody needed to know."

Previous academic research has shown the power of television to evoke emotion,[2] but how this might be accomplished may take many forms.

"It was not so much that I felt we needed to reassure everybody and keep them from panicking, but I just felt the best way, the most responsible thing to do, was to try to make sure we gave them the occasional big picture," said Al Ortiz, executive producer of special events at CBS.

On the other hand, some journalists did note they paid special attention to the tone they adopted on 9/11, and they were aware of the impact they might have on viewers—and some admitted that they had to fight their own emotions to keep calm.

"You just wanted to throw up your hands and say everybody go home now because the world has ended," said Jon Scott of FOX News. "At some point, and I can't tell you when this happened, but it occurred to me that if everybody did play Chicken Little, then the terrorists won, and that was exactly what they were trying to do."

Gary Tuchman, national correspondent for CNN, said he paid serious attention to his tone and to his demeanor on 9/11.

"People are at home thinking the world might be coming to an end," he said. "If you're carrying on, people are going to think things are still going on. People watching on TV, if they see you're calm at the scene, they'll calm down, too."

And Molly Falconer of FOX News admitted her concern about how she appeared as a television journalist: "I had a gas mask hanging around my neck, and I actually purposely did not put it on when I probably should have had it on," she said, referring to coverage from the scene of 9/11 after the towers had fallen. "I had a paper mask on for a couple of shots and the gas mask on for a couple of shots, but the majority of time I didn't have it on because I felt like that looked kind of sensational,"

Bill Shine, also of FOX News, gave a different reason for wanting to keep calm.

"The first thing you don't want to do as a human being on a day like September 11 is add to it. You don't want to add to the terror. You don't want to put misinformation out and scare people for any reason."

Shepard Smith of FOX News at one point told his audience to just find a loved one to hug. He explained his thinking.

"It just became so painfully clear," he said, "that we didn't know where we were or where we were going. We had no idea how much of an attack was left. It just felt like the only thing I could contribute at the moment was that. And, I think that was more self-defense for me as much as for anyone else. It was very unsettling, an unsettling time. All I wanted to do was hug somebody I loved."

Keeping the Emotion Hidden

Reporters are taught to be above the fray, bemused gods on Olympus watching with curiosity the triumphs and tragedies occurring below. They are told in school and in the newsroom that their jobs simply are to report the facts without opinion. They are tossed onto beats in their first jobs where they must face up, often daily, to the brutal deaths of others by traffic accident or through human rage. They are monitored daily, both internally by their bosses and externally by their audiences, to insure they hew closely to this journalistic standard. Those who learn how to appear concerned but not affected by death in its raw form are rewarded by promotion.

Most television journalists never had faced a test like that of 9/11. The domestic terror of the 1995 Oklahoma City bombing was their only recent reference point. But Oklahoma City occurred all at once, not in a series of events strung out over several hours, and Oklahoma City, to most national reporters, occurred to someone else's neighbors.

As for Pearl Harbor, the 1941 bombing was an entry in history books, an event that occurred before the first commercial television signal was broadcast, an event in which violence was inflicted by combatants on combatants, not on the friends and neighbors who had waved earlier this morning as they left the commuter train that brought them into the city.

Reporters who covered 9/11 returned to this theme repeatedly as they described what went through their minds in the early stages of the catastrophe. Their country had just been attacked; their friends, or friends of friends, had just been killed; their president was on the run, flitting from air force base to air force base around the country; their leaders were in hiding; and their government was in confusion. And yet, reporters were to show little emotion, to be impartial, impassive observers dedicated to reporting the truth.

Walking that line was nearly impossible. And some journalists said walking the line wasn't even necessary on 9/11, that the nature of the act made impartiality unnecessary.

The reaction of reporters fell into two broad categories. One group took the position that everyone expected reporters to have some emotion and patriotism, given the events of the day. The key was limiting how much of that showed on camera and not allowing that emotion to interfere with the job that had to be done.

"I don't see that it is our job to necessarily wave the flag," said Marcy McGinnis, CBS News, in a comment that echoed this group's thinking.

"It is our job to tell the news and tell the facts.... I mean, it is sort of an understood. Nobody is not (patriotic)."

Robert Dembo, head of the national news assignment desk at NBC, said the issue was not the emotion felt by journalists and not whether they were patriotic but whether they showed it on camera.

"The question, I think, is whether it is appropriate for journalists ... to wear it on their sleeve to the degree that they did, or that some did on that day," Dembo said. "I think there was a degree of jingoistic flag waving, heart beating, go get 'em, cheerleading that I saw on some networks. It is one thing to be a patriot. It is another thing to wear your patriotism on your sleeve.

"You know, I did not drape my desk with American flags even though it is on camera. I did not do those things. It is not appropriate even though the United States may be attacked. It is our role to remain as objective as we possibly can, and I think we did. And I think that when you put, if you slap a flag on your vest, it is making it very difficult to certainly appear to be objective, let alone to be objective."

A second group argued journalists had a right to show emotion, and the public expected them to react as Americans first and reporters second.

Shepard Smith, of FOX News, summed up this group's thinking by saying: "I felt like it was an OK time to be an American. It seemed to me that it was OK that we needed something around which to rally, and that was what jumped out for all of us. I didn't know what other people were doing. It just made sense to me that this was not a two-sided argument, not in that microcosm down there."

Lester Holt, news anchor for *MSNBC News*, said the one-sidedness of the story made it easier to show emotion.

"There is a time that I think it is OK to be human," Holt said. "This was a story that didn't have two sides to it. You didn't have to worry about being impartial. So it was OK to be factual but at the same time it was OK to show some emotion. I'm not necessarily talking about blubbering on the air, but you know, if you tear up, it was OK.

"I think sometimes (when) we get out of journalism school, we are like 'I am a journalist and I am not affected by anything.' Well, you know what, you are also a human being, and you were affected."

Paul Friedman, executive vice president, ABC, said it was almost impossible to avoid patriotism in the coverage: "The patriotism kind of became part of the story. The flags came out instantly. The singing of 'God Bless America' started instantly. It was hard to avoid."

Polls Show Public Angry over Attack

How successful the media were in calming the nation's fears—if, indeed, that happened—is an open question. A poll conducted by the National Opinion Research Center between Sept. 13 and Sept. 27, 2001, found the dominant emotion to be not fear but anger. It also showed that Americans reacted to 9/11 with less emotion than they did to the news of the assassination of John F. Kennedy thirty-eight years earlier. For example, 50.6 percent of those surveyed after 9/11 reported feeling nervous and tense compared to 68 percent reporting that emotion in 1963.[3]

As a contrary viewpoint, another poll, this taken by the Pew Center between Sept. 11 and Sept. 15, found that 71 percent of Americans surveyed felt depressed. Pew did not poll for anger in that survey, but a second poll taken Oct. 1-3 found that 71 percent of those surveyed said they were angry about the attacks.[4]

Earlier research also has shown media to be effective in guiding people—telling them what to do in a crisis or disaster—and in helping the process by providing consolation.[5] This research states that the media, apart from transmitting information, also have a "social utility" function that refers to the use of the media to fulfill needs—perhaps companionship and emotional support—other than the need for information.[6]

If television had a consoling effect, perhaps it was because television is accepted as an entertainment medium that provides a fantasy world into which the public willingly enters. Several journalists hinted at this in interviews. Jim Murphy, executive producer of the *CBS Evening News*, for example, was one who mentioned the impact of the television set in normalizing the abnormal, "One of the good things about what we did was by putting the whole thing into a little box and making it into a TV show, we also gave you the sense that this is just what happens in the world," he said. "This is one of those things that happens. This is history in the making. This is a big story, yeah, but ... we are not all dead. Society didn't come to an end; it is not over. These things come and go...."

But normalizing the abnormal is just one part of what television news does. It also may blur the lines between the real and virtual worlds by using the same techniques for news as are used for entertainment.

Steve Friedman, senior executive producer for the *Early Show* on CBS, noted the similarities between making good television news and making good television.

"I am thinking pace. I am thinking style. I'm thinking how to move it, how to make it the most interesting thing, because people in a crisis always switch, and I figure that eventually they will get to us and I want them when they get to us to stay," he said.

This doesn't mean, of course, that television news is dominated by the same considerations as television entertainment. But it does mean that television news producers must react to what people expect from television. News packaged without style or pacing or production values would attract little audience in today's fast-paced, graphics-intensive media world.

"Television has a few ways to do things," Friedman noted. "There is the reporter in the field, there is the interview, and then there are the reports. And my job when I do breaking coverage is to mix and match, and I make (it all) into the best television I can.

"So I don't put in all the phone calls, I don't put all the reports together, I don't put all the interviews together. I go from one to the other to the other to the other to make it as dynamic as I can because I am a television producer," he said. "Sure, we are journalists. Sure, we want to get the information out. But I want you, once we've got you, to stay here. I don't want you to go to NBC, I don't want you to go to ABC, I don't want you to go to CNN."

A third factor was at work on the morning of 9/11 that further blurred the distinctions between reality and virtual. Nobody really expected 9/11. The unexpectedness of the event, heightened by the unreality that is television, created a feeling of surrealism. Eric Shawn of FOX News spent the first two hours in the studio on 9/11. He remembers how watching 9/11 on the television monitors affected him.

"It was very surreal because I wasn't seeing the building in person like other people," he said. "Since it was on TV, it had that disaster movie quality to it."

Whatever the reasons and whatever the circumstances as journalists went about doing what journalists do, however, this study confirms that the public came away from the results of journalists' work with positive feelings.

Information Is the Greatest Public Need

Among those reasons for the public's positive response, perhaps the major one, was that they were getting the information they needed to understand the situation. More than 80 percent of the stories were identified predominantly as focusing presentation of facts, while 14.8 percent of stories were primarily analytical. The coverage specifically devoted to guiding the audience in a crisis situation (1.3 percent) and to consolation or easing stress and anxiety of audience (2 percent) was negligible. And, looking at the changes of media functions by stage of crisis, no changes were found. An average of 81 percent of the stories was presented as fact across three stages of the crisis.

That was the general pattern, but networks did differ. FOX News provided, by far, the highest number of stories that could be coded as guiding or consolation, with 6.79 percent of its stories falling into those two categories. CNN followed with 4.11 percent of its stories in the first twenty-four hours focusing on such content. In contrast, only 1.17 percent of the stories appearing on NBC News in the first twenty-four hours focused on consolation or guiding.

The most significant difference probably was in the number of guiding stories. Guiding stories totaled 1.17 percent of the stories that were seen on network and cable television in the first twenty-four hours. Guiding stories hit a high of 2.7 percent in the first three hours of the crisis and then dropped sharply, ending up in single digits for most of the cycle. The percentage of guiding stories would have been far lower had it not been for FOX News, which totaled 2.91 percent and CNN, which came in at 1.98 percent. The three broadcast networks devoted less than 1 percent of their coverage to stories that could be considered guiding in nature.

The higher percentages for consolation and guiding stories by the cable operations could be a function of the difference in the way cable and networks operate normally. Cable operates much like a wire service, and production is geared toward feeding the appetite of a 24-hour monster. Its reporters and editors are accustomed to a fast-paced world of media in which more content is needed and little time is available for packaging. The focus is on producing news events and getting them on the air as quickly as possible. Network news operations, in contrast, are geared toward producing a show once every twenty-four hours. Instead of reporting individual stories and putting them immediately on the air, their producers tend to think more in terms of packaging to produce a coherent whole.

The higher percentages also could be factors of available resources. Consolation and guiding stories are easier than hard news stories to produce. The networks had a clear advantage in terms of available resources. All three have headquarters in New York City and were able to throw news teams from the morning show as well as the evening news into the coverage. In contrast, CNN is headquartered in Atlanta although it does have a substantive bureau in New York, and its resources—cameras and trucks as well as staff members—had to be physically transported into a city that was quickly closed to air transport.

However, difference was found in the coverage devoted to consolation. Almost no stories were devoted to consolation during the first stage of the crisis. As the coverage continued, stories of consolation increased to 2.78 percent in the second stage, between 11 a.m. and 3 p.m., hit a high of 3.5 percent in hours of 3 p.m. to 7 p.m. and then dropped to 2.92 percent from 7 p.m. until midnight.

This factor perhaps could be explained by the nature of the event itself. The lack of stories devoted to consolation and guidance may have been simply a result of the enormity of the event and the fact that it consumed all available human resources in the two media capitals of the nation.

This explanation also would be consistent with the study's finding of a lack of analysis in the first twenty-four hours of coverage. Normally, twenty-four-hour coverage would be replete with analysis. Analysis is normally used to fill the time between developments in the breaking news, to keep the viewer engaged while reporters search for new information or new persons to interview. After all, anchors cannot just keep repeating the same information over and over without losing audience share. That pattern exhibited itself during the first and second stages of coverage, in the time from 8 a.m. until 3 p.m., as reporters and editors tried to determine what had happened and who might be involved. But in this case analysis began dropping after 3 p.m. and stayed low for the rest of the twenty-four-hour period, having been replaced by an extremely heavy dose of facts.

"What We Do Is Valuable"

It would be a mistake to draw too many sweeping conclusions from the content analysis of 9/11. This was an anomaly by any standard, disaster coverage on a scale never before seen or attempted. Nothing since the 1941 bombings of Pearl Harbor compared in scope or impact on the nation. To say that 9/11 was television without a safety net is an understatement. Television has operated without a safety net many times in covering past disasters, but never before in a theater this big and on a story this huge.

Interviews confirmed that journalists felt overwhelmed by the rapid succession of facts. News managers had little time to ponder questions such as balance, fairness, and consolation because they were too busy getting equipment and reporters in place, coordinating film and sound reports not just from the scene but from around the world, setting up hotel beds where tired journalists could crash for a few hours and handling phone calls from worried spouses.

"I barely remember a damn thing because it was just too intense," said Jim Murphy, executive producer of the *CBS Evening News*. "I actually think it is one of the reasons that it (9/11) didn't seem to have the personal impact on me that it probably should have had. I was just too damn busy to notice."

But Murphy does remember one thing about 9/11 with a degree of pride.

"It proved that what we do is important," he said. "It proved that what we do is vital. It proved that what we do is valuable and that it matters. I mean what would people have done without that information and without being able to turn on their TVs and see it and hear it? So it was great to see that we were really a part of the fabric of the society and that we mattered to it.

"Maybe that is making too much out of it. I don't know. It sure felt that way, and it felt good to know you were working on something that people had to have."

Notes

1.   Graber, D. A. (1980). *Mass Media and American Politics*. Washington DC: Congressional Quarterly Press, p. 228.
2.   Nimmo, D., & Combs, J.E. (1985). *Nightly Horrors: Crisis Coverage in Television Network News,* Knoxville, TN: The University of Tennessee Press.
3.   Smith, T.W., Rasinski, K. A., & Toce, M. (Oct. 25, 2001). America Rebounds: A National Study of Public Response to the September 11th Terrorist Attacks, the National Opinion Research Center. Retrieved on April 13, 2008, from *http://www. norc.uchicago.edu/projects/reaction/pubresp.pdf.*
4.   Pew Research Center for the People and the Press (September 19, 2001). American Psyche Reeling from Terror Attack, Pew Research Center. Retrieved on April 13, 2008, from *http://people-press.org/reports/display.php3?ReportID=3.*
5.   Graber, D. A. (1980). *Mass Media and American Politics.*; Schramm, W. (1965). Communication in Crisis. In B.S. Greenberg & E. B. Parker (Eds.): *The Kennedy Assassination and the American Public: Social Communication in Crises* (p. 1-25). Stanford, CA: Stanford University Press.
6.   Dominick, J. R. (1996). *The Dynamics of Mass Communication.* New York: McGraw-Hill.

5

Journalistic Norms: The Media as Shepherd

Kirsten Mogensen

ABC correspondent Don Dahler lived near the World Trade Center in New York City. He was surprised on September 11, 2001, to hear a flight close by, so he rushed to the window, but even before he got there, he heard the huge explosion. The sound reminded him of a missile. Looking out, he saw a gigantic hole in the tower.

Immediately he grabbed a phone, called ABC's news desk, and moments later he was on the air. Most of the morning, he reported via telephone from his fire escape.

Dahler compared his role on September 11 to that of the famous American radio reporter Edward R. Murrow, who reported from London during World War II:

"I had become a radio reporter at that point. I didn't have a camera. I was, you know, Murrow on the rooftops of London trying to relay back to the American listeners exactly what was happening in as descriptive and yet, not melodramatic, language as possible. I would try to just give it as succinct and clear a description as possible."

Meanwhile, at CNN's headquarters, approximately forty people had gathered for the daily editorial meeting in the conference room at 8.30 a.m. and an equal number of senior staff participated by telephone. They were discussing the major stories of the day when the deputy bureau chief in New York, Edith Chapin, jumped on the line and said: "We have breaking news. An airplane has crashed into the World Trade Center!"

Senior Vice President and National Managing Editor Keith McAllister later said: "Everyone in the room, without a word being spoken, instantly got to their feet and started running downstairs to the newsroom. It was literally all 40 people leapt to their feet and piled out of the room and ran downstairs, and we all kind of took our positions in the newsroom."

The scene was repeated in newsrooms across the nation. At first, reporters treated the news as an accident, but after the second crash, most instinctively knew it was terrorism and what was expected of them.

Thirty-seven of these journalists who covered 9/11 for the major American networks and cable networks were asked to describe their work on that day. And as they did, some seemingly shared professional norms and values emerged.

Norms in this case means shared understanding of how journalists ought to react in a situation of acute national crisis. They do not include technical patterns, normal habits or acts meant to satisfy the individual journalist's biological or psychological needs such as eating and sleeping.[1] Professional norms develop as professionals try to solve ethical problems that by their very nature are specific to the profession.[2] Professionals decide how to behave in a given situation by drawing on experience from previous situations. Swedish scholar Sven Ove Hansson writes that "informal normative notions are quite complex and have meaning components related to agency, possibility, commitment, conditionality, defeasibility, the application of rules, etc."[3]

According to legal philosopher Alf Ross, norms have a binding force if a person in a given situation "feels a special prompting or impulse to act according to the pattern. This impulse does not appear as a manifestation of his needs and interests; it may, indeed, conflict with these." When asked to explain behavior, the person will use words like "obligation," "duty," or "ought to."[4] A norm may be in force within a profession even though not every single individual within the group reacts in accordance with the norm or supports it.[5]

Journalists interviewed for this study talked in terms of duty and obligation, to be certain. They also talked about how this belief in duty created tension within them, of general uneasiness, and a persistent sense of being unsettled.

"That first few weeks, I was incredibly edgy," said Jim Murphy, executive producer for *CBS Evening News*. "I didn't sleep much and lived through this freaking horror. I worked my ass off. You know, you just were worried that something terrible was going to happen. Nothing mattered more than doing your job well."

And Don Dahler had this perspective: "The vast majority of the journalists who went running down to that site and to their job did not go running down there willingly thinking that they were going to be glorified in that endeavor. They went running there because it was their job. Many of them were at great personal risk, and yet they did it."

Many talked about how they worked twenty-four hours or more before they had a chance to sleep. They said no one complained even though some nearly died when the towers fell; others refused to leave the newsroom despite bomb threats; all rotated no matter how big they were as stars, and nobody cared about lack of proper food or other conveniences.

"I think everybody would do it again," said Jonathan Wald, executive producer for NBC's *Today Show*. "That's a selflessness that we all feel about getting our jobs done. And you know we all make huge sacrifices for our jobs constantly. And that's a given part of the job."

The consensus corresponded with description provided by scholars of a "compulsion" experienced by people who react to the binding force of norms. This study of television coverage of 9/11 translated those norms into ten characteristics of crisis reporting, supported by quotes taken from the interview transcripts.

Norm 1: Journalism Is a Public Service

The journalists who covered 9/11 generally were proud of what they believed to be an important "public service" or a "national service" in which they acted in the "public interest" and were a real "part of the fabric of the society." Many referred to their jobs that day as a "duty," which they were happy to have been able to fulfill. For example, Paul Slavin, executive producer at ABC *World News Tonight*, said about reporting during national crisis: "What we are doing is as important as any organization within the government."

NBC News Correspondent Rehema Ellis compared the role of journalists to that of fire fighters:

> Journalists do what firefighters do every day. Where they stand and walk into burning buildings. And they don't know the people inside, but they put themselves into harm's way and jeopardize their own personal safety in order to help someone.

The interviewees believed they worked on behalf of viewers.

"There was this sense of what comes out of my mouth and out of our reporting is going to affect hundreds of millions of people around the world who have got to be watching now," said *FOX News* anchor Shepard Smith.

A public service of this nature was rewarded by the viewers in their evaluations.[6] Anchor Matt Lauer, *The Today Show* on NBC, learned about the viewers' satisfaction directly:

I don't think I have ever been more proud to be in this business than I was in the aftermath of September 11th. I can't tell you the number of people who, whether they watched ABC, NBC, CBS, would come up to us on the street and just say thank you. It is an enormous reminder of what the media can mean to a country and to people all around the world at a time of crisis.

Norm 2: Viewers Need Information Quickly and Accurately

Journalists at the major TV networks saw it as their mission to provide information quickly. They believed the viewers needed this information to cope with the tensions of the insecure situation.

"The motivation of the network is to tell the news as accurately, as fairly, objectively and as quickly as possible. I mean that's always been our mission," said Slavin.

All the major networks and cable networks televised live pictures from the scene of disaster within fifteen minutes after American Airlines Flight 11 slammed into the North Tower at 8:45 a.m. Executive Producer and Director Al Ortiz, CBS Special Events, explained that with crisis coverage "you just go on the air and hold it for as long as you can and the news gathering part of the organization goes into high gear."

The newsgathering aimed at providing a "running river" of answers to what happened, Bill Felling, national editor at CBS, said, and it was organized in a way that made this flood as fast and smooth as possible. As an illustrative example, McAllister emphasized the importance of eye contact in the newsroom: "The speed at which you are doing it matters on breaking news. You really got to look at somebody, hear their voice."

Anchor Lester Holt, MSNBC, mentioned an online flight explorer program that made it possible for viewers to keep track of how many planes were in the air at a given time and how the number gradually emptied out. Vice President William O. Wheatley, NBC News, simply noted that "it is almost always reassuring when you present people with information that keeps up to the minute as to what's going on."

And Lauer explained why the viewers needed the information: "You need to get them information that there aren't any other guided missiles out there heading in their direction."

The journalists emphasized that the information had to be correct. Ortiz explained that wrong information could scare relatives unnecessarily: "It mattered a great deal if you reported the wrong aircraft, right? Because everybody was worrying about whether somebody they knew was on the airplane."

Norm 3: Honesty is the Best Policy

When CNN started its crisis coverage from the World Trade Center at 8.49.50, Anchor Carol Lin told the viewers she did not know what happened:

> This is just in. You are looking at obviously a very disturbing live shot there. That is the World Trade Center, and we have unconfirmed reports this morning that a plane has crashed into one of the towers of the World Trade Center. CNN Center right now is just beginning to work on this story, obviously calling our sources and trying to figure out exactly what happened.[7]

Within minutes the networks, MSNBC and FOX News also televised live shots without knowing exactly what had happened.

Journalists showed respect for the viewers by (1) being open about what they did not know; (2) telling the viewers whether information was confirmed; and (3) correcting wrong information as soon as possible. On September 11, few had correct information initially about what happened. Journalists received incorrect information from seemingly trustworthy sources such as rescue personal and public officials.

Delivering unconfirmed information was a craft in itself. Senior Vice President Marcy McGinnis, CBS News, cited the comments of then-Anchor Dan Rather as an example of how to handle this.

"Dan is very good. If there is some rumor that is being reported by somebody else, or some fact that might be reported by somebody else and we don't have it yet on our own, he'll say: 'You may be hearing from other sources that there might be planes in the air, but we do not know this for a fact. Our people are checking it out, and you can be assured we will tell you the facts when we know them.'"

At Ground Zero, the reporters explained to the viewers how difficult it was to obtain solid information. Tuchman expressed it as a norm: "Be bluntly honest with the viewers, explain the process. Explain that there's a lot of commotion and chaos. And while you're staying calm, explain: 'We're trying to gather the information the best we can. We're gonna give it to you as it comes.'"

Transparency provided viewers with an insight that made it easier for them to judge the performance of their news channel and may have limited the breeding ground for conspiracy theories.

"The man behind the curtain, I think, was very much more visible now than maybe it really ever has been," said Dan Dahler. "And that's not a bad thing. I think we'd benefit from more of that because I think the public would be less inclined to suspect that we make things up."

Norm 4: We're All in This Together

When the anchors explained to the viewers what they did not know, it worked as an appeal to viewers who had relevant information to share. Networks and cable networks then became information centers, collecting information from single viewers and broadcasting it to the mass of viewers. In other words, they made on-air research. All the networks benefited from this give-and-take with the viewers. As an example, all networks interviewed eyewitnesses to the events. As another example, CBS received a tip from an anonymous viewer regarding the names of some of the known terrorists who had boarded the flights. National Editor William Felling, CBS:

> This is one of the classic pieces of fabulous news gathering. It is almost serendipitous, but nothing is serendipitous in news. It comes from good skills, good practices. Good anonymous phone calls often are right.

However, as is the case with other norms, use of the public in the research had its limits. The problem was that not all callers were serious, well-informed viewers wanting to share information. Some were mentally sick people hoping for attention, some were relatives and rescue workers driven by hopes, others tried to scare the public even more by calling in bomb threats. Involving the public then implied careful source evaluation and pre-interviews.

Norm 5: We Cannot Show Emotion

Journalists were expected to remain calm and professional on the air during the crisis no matter how shocked and fearful they were. McGinnis: "When you are in this business, you have to maintain calm. You have to be almost like a doctor is in an operating room. They are trained to be calm so that when they open the guy's chest and the heart, they don't freak out."

Anchor Jon Scott, FOX News, described the conflict between his personal feelings of fear and his professional role:

> There was a time when I just wanted to throw up my hands and say: "This is terrible." I just want to crawl under the desk now! But that's what the terrorist wanted; they wanted to shut us down as a nation. Just have us stop everything and crawl under the covers, and at some point I determined that we weren't going to do that.

Three of the interviewees used the fairytale figure Chicken Little as metaphor for undesired behavior. One of them was Lauer, who described viewers' reactions as one of the rewards for professional behavior: "People were very impressed by the fact that we did not start Chicken Little. It is not the end of the world. Even though we may have thought that way."

Also encouraging were the stories, which professional colleagues told about the heroes of the business. Such stories emphasized important norms and values. One such hero-story concerned NBC Correspondent Jim Miklaszewski. He broadcast from his office in the Pentagon, when American Airlines Flight 77 had just crashed into the other end of that building. Wheatley was impressed: "If you go back and look at that tape, he's hardly rattled by it. He's trying to tell you what went on. He's making calls from his desk in the Pentagon."

Other normative stories circulating implied the results when journalists behave like Chicken Little. As an example one such anti-hero story told about a reporter, who had been on air when an earthquake hit twenty years earlier. Executive Producer Shelley Ross, *Good Morning America*, ABC: "He went under his desk, and his life and his career was dramatically altered for a while, because he made everybody panic. You can't have somebody who jumps under the desk too soon."

Alternatively, Ross described a colleague this way: "He is Mr. Cool. He is who you want in the control room with you in a time like this."

Journalists who stayed professional were preferred anywhere in the organizations. In relation to coverage of 9/11, some employees resigned from their jobs at the TV organizations because they could not handle the conflict between personal feelings and professional roles. For journalists, the challenge of September 11 was an unexpected test of their abilities to do the job. McGinnis explained:

> This is the kind of story that will propel your career to new heights on one hand or break you on another hand. And it is just the nature of the business. You find out what you are made of in a story like this.

Norm 6: Reassurance Is a By-Product of Journalism

Journalists sought to present information that was reassuring such as press conferences with government officials or stories about the bravery of rescue workers and about the humanity expressed by people. One may discuss whether they aimed at reassurance or whether reassurance was a by-product. Wheatley: "It's rarely ever our business to reassure the nation. Our business is to bring in the information. Now if that information is reassuring, that's the way it should be."

However, in the newsroom at FOX News, the leaders talked about the need to "restore calm" in the first hours after the terror attack on World Trade Center, and Anchor John Gibson said later: "The idea that we had to reassure the nation was implicit. The island was not sinking; everybody didn't die."

Michael Rosen, senior producer, ABC Special Events, explained what type of information would be reassuring:

> Viewers needed to be assured that the country was not falling apart, needed to be reassured that the institutions were stable. When you see people running out of the White House, you have to assure people that there is a plan, and that there's a safe room, and the president is safe. When you see the Pentagon smoking, you have to assure people that the defense of the country is still intact and you can still defend the country.

Murphy explained that the media in themselves have a reassuring function:

> One of the good things about what we did was by putting the whole thing into a little box and making it into a TV show. We gave you the sense that this is just what happens in the world. This is a big story, but we are not all dead. Society didn't come to an end.

The word *reassuring* was used by several of the interviewees as was the word *comfort*. As an example, Tuchman said: "You can't ask for anything else in a career: Doing something like this: To be able to get comfort to a nation and a world, in some way."

And, according to journalists, the viewers seemed to appreciate that role of television. Lauer: "People were very thankful for the fact that we tried to keep them comforted in knowing that, 'OK, this probably isn't the end of the world.'"

However, neither reassurance nor comfort ought to be provided on the expense of truth. The situation could be compared to that of police telling parents that one of their children died in an accident. It did not help to hide the truth, but journalists were aware that the message could be delivered together with an expression of compassion. As Jon Scott of FOX News said: "I just wanted to sort of do whatever I could to buck people up."

Norm 7: Sensationalism Is Normal; Downplay the Sensational

Sensation is among the news criteria in journalism, and the events on September 11, 2001, were certainly sensational. They were in fact so scaring and shocking that by instinct journalists chose to tell the story in a less shocking way than the footage may have called for. The crisis format included long-distance rather than close-up shots; verbal descriptions rather than visuals; abstract rather than concrete terms; rational rather than emotional statements. In other words, they used to some extent a format known by journalists to limit identification and emotional impact. Tuchman: "You want to tell the truth, but you don't want to make people so sick they can't watch it."

This norm was to be understood as relative. The coverage was shocking enough for the viewers,[8] and one in ten felt the coverage should be less sensational in nature. [9]

During our interviews most journalists spontaneously provided examples of pictures, words or information they found questionable, including footage of people burning to death or jumping to death from the burning towers; close-up footage of the cloud of debris from the tower because it contained remains; information about bomb-threats; replay of footage showing the flights slam into the towers; information about the rescue workers collecting body parts during the night; description of body parts including torsos, arms and feet; questioning victims about whether they heard other people scream or die; close-up footage of victims covered in blood; and visuals showing the journalists with gas masks.

However, the top people at the networks and cable networks disagreed about the extent to which the viewers wanted to see certain footage, and each said they had been involved in ongoing discussions about the tone and the ethical questions related to horrifying footage and information.

The reasons for the norm can be divided into two groups: (1) the need to present the information in a way that allowed the viewers to watch without being overwhelmed; and (2) respect for the victims and their relatives.

With regard to the first, journalists saw the footage coming into the control room or saw what happened at Ground Zero. Even though they were highly experienced journalists, they were personally affected by the footage and used their own reactions to measure what viewers could handle. *NBC Nightly News* Executive Producer Stephen Capus:

> We made a decision not to air footage of people committing suicide from the top of those buildings, and those images haunt me to this day. Because I saw them come into the control room. And they took your breath away. I didn't feel we needed to show that.

Steve Friedman, senior executive producer at CBS for *The Early Show*, among others, did not find that the viewers needed to see close up pictures of the horror:

Are you going to show dead people burning up? People know what it is. You don't have to show it to them. Are you going to show what a burnt body looks like? Or to show somebody riving in pain dying? It is not television!

On the other hand, the journalists agreed that the viewers needed to know what happened. Lauer discussed the fact that some disturbing pictures were broadcast during the live coverage:

I did not think that that was something we needed necessarily to shy away from. I thought it was the story. You know you aren't going to scare people any more than they have already been scared September 11th.

With regard to the second reason—respect for the victims and their relatives—this is also relative. Scott described the form of sensationalizing which was not accepted:

With the lenses we have these days you could zoom in and pick out a face. You know you would be able to see: "Oh, there is daddy up there on the 102nd floor!" And you just don't need to put those kinds of shots on TV, in my opinion.

However, journalists also knew that they could not present a truthful coverage if they dealt only with the wishes of the victims and their relatives. McGinnis:

You can't broadcast news only with the victims in mind. Otherwise you'd never show anything. Every major breaking story that involves a tragedy has victims, and the victims are traumatized by it, and if they had their way, they'd never see it again because it only brings up all of these horrible memories.

Norm 8: Avoid the Extremists

One professional norm is to make sure the coverage is objective, fair, balanced.[10] The SPJ Code of Ethics states, among other norms, that journalists should "Tell the story of the diversity and magnitude of the human experience boldly, even when it is unpopular to do so." "Examining their own cultural values and avoid imposing those values on others," and "Support the open exchange of views, even views they find repugnant."

While journalists who covered 9/11 supported these norms in general, content analyses of CNN's coverage the first twenty-four hours showed that American sources primarily expressed mainstream opinions. Extremist views were expressed only by people outside the USA, creating an illusion of a coherent USA faced with a diverse and chaotic world.[11] But some Americans did have extremist views, including people expressing support for the terrorists[12] and others expressing general hate for Muslims and Arabs.[13] Such views were referred to in the news coverage, but the American extremists had little opportunity to explain their views directly to the public on national television the first twenty-four hours.

Interesting consequences of letting people outside the nation express the magnitude of views were that the American viewers became informed about major viewpoints and ideas in accordance with the theories of social responsibility[14] while such repugnant views presented from a far distance seemed less threatening than if the same views had been expressed by people in the neighborhood. In Figure 5.1 the shaded areas illustrate the segments which primarily supplied sources to national television the first 24 hours:

Figure 5.1

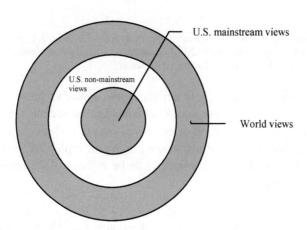

Note: U.S. mainstream opinions were voiced in American television on September 11 - 12 as were the diversity of opinions coming from the world community. However, provoking or extremist opinions voiced by the American community were not present on the air the first twenty-four hours after the terror attacks.

Several of our journalist interviewees implied that Americans supporting the terrorists did not express legitimate views, and terrorism was in fact illegal according to international law.[15] Tuchman, as an example, made implicit reference to international law in the following statement:

"Objectivity is important, but when you are attacked, you don't say: 'Well here are the two sides to the story.' This was an attack on civilians.

Attacks on civilians are never permitted, not in any time. There are no two sides to that; it's a horrible thing."

Journalists also took into consideration that their viewers were in a state of shock and fear. Murphy:

> You have to be concerned about how the whole country is reacting and what they are dealing with. I mean it was a huge trauma. So you couldn't just immediately go out and say on the first day: "Good evening, this was probably your fault, the history of western civilization has led to a complete dismissal of the Islamic world and its culture, and it decided to strike back." You can't do that; you wouldn't want to do that. It wouldn't be right. It also wouldn't be objective either.

Among the diversity of opinions reported from outside the USA was footage of Palestinians cheering in the street, and national television showed that even though the Palestine authorities had asked news media not to broadcast it.[16] Bill Shine, network executive producer, FOX News:

> That tape, I think, gave Americans another aspect: that there are people out there who think today is a great day. Maybe everybody should pay attention here because there are people cheering what happened today.

Shine referred implicitly to a norm from normative press theory that states that journalists ought to warn citizens against serious threats.[17] The terrorists themselves—dead or alive—of course had access to national television through the intensive coverage and replay of their attacks. Journalists considered their attacks to be a form of communication. Friedman explained:

> These guys blew up the World Trade Center for the pictures because they knew it was going to be on CNN. I am so cynical about these guys; I believed they attacked at a time when they knew all three network morning shows were going to be on live. So they knew they would get live coverage right away.

Norm 9: Avoid Stereotypes

When terrorists or foreign nations attack, journalists are instantly aware of the fact that the shock, fear, and anger among citizens may easily develop into backlash against innocent people of the same race or nationality as the attackers. And, according to the professional norms the news reports should never inflame. McAllister: "There you feel a sense of proactive obligation. We've been down this road as a society before and seen what happens."

Some of the interviewees talked about a formula for crisis coverage, and Lauer said the awareness of possible backlash was included in the mental list among professionals: "There are like 10 things that come into play immediately when a news story breaks, and that's one of them these days."

However several of the journalists said informants saw fewer problems with backlash related to the events of 9/11 than what might have been expected. Murphy:

> I am also sort of impressed that the backlash didn't seem to me to be anywhere near as severe as you might expect it to be when people are reacting with really strong emotions. So, to some extent, I sort of felt a little bit proud of my country, even though I know that there are lots of people in this country that are pretty bigoted.

The journalists pointed to three communication strategies that might have helped limit backlash: (1) statements from government officials; (2) concern about the tone used in this case when describing Muslims and Arabs; (3) commitment to the truth.

Since journalists normally distinguish between news and commentaries[18] and prefer to provide news reporting, they were thankful that President George W. Bush and other government officials quickly made statements about avoiding the tendency to single out Arab-Americans or to blame all Arabs for the attacks.

Concerns about the tone used by the journalists were based on experience from previous events, ongoing professional discussions about the manner in which Muslims and Islam were portrayed, and general knowledge about the history of America, including the unfair treatment of American Japanese following the bombing of Pearl Harbor in the Second World War.

However, the reason for the norm was a commitment to the truth, which also meant that journalists would cover only stories that met normal news criteria. McAllister explained the news values in the stories about American Arabs and Muslims:

> There was a story to cover. There was inappropriate racial profile going on. There was a real issue about the extent of the FBI sweeping the country, there was some real acts of discrimination occurring, some of them violent. The retaliation against Muslims in this country was a story that had started happening across the country right away, and it needed to be covered. And so, we covered it. I mean there are people getting hurt.

The same commitment to truth also meant that they would not suppress relevant information even though it could harm the image of Muslims or Arabs. McGinnis:

> We don't want to be a bunch of censors who want to protect the American people from the news. I also think that you have to give the American people a little credit for being able to understand what they are watching. I mean everybody who is watching is not going to run out and react on a level that is going to cause somebody else harm. Basically, they want information, and I think the more information you give, the better informed the public is. Our job is to inform them, not to protect them from that stuff.

Slavin summarized the norm: "Not only was it an attempt to minimize but it was an attempt to make sure that accurate information was out there"

Norm 10: Find the Good among the Bad

According to Johan Galtung and Marie Holmboe Ruge (1965), the more negative the consequences of an event, the more likely it will be covered by news media. The terror attacks on September 11 were bad news and received maximum coverage twenty-four hours a day for a week. However, it was interesting to note that the coverage also contained a great number of reports about the courtesy, help, and courage shown by individuals. Galtung & Ruge wrote that the more unexpected the news was, the better the chances for coverage. During a disaster, good news stands out as unexpected.

"When you're walking through a darkened street, and there's a house with the light on, that's what you notice," Dahler said.

> So you might say there are other things going on in the dark, but what catches your attention and what focuses you is that light in that house. My job was to report on the scene on the Ground Zero itself. And the light of Ground Zero, the predominant story was the people—not just the firemen and the rescue workers and the policemen who ran into the buildings and then lost their lives because of those acts of heroism, but the rescue workers who worked the debris pile and were constantly injured. That was a news judgment that was so easy to make. There was no other story than that to my mind down there. It was one of the best things I've ever seen in my life, so that's what you want to convey to the people. That becomes the big story.

However, the limit of this norm is again the truth that, according to our interviewees, cannot be compromised.

Development of Professional Norms

Journalists at national television networks said they reacted by instinct when the news about the terror attacks broke,[19] but during the interviews it became evident that the instinct was based on a significant knowledge about public affairs as well as professional norms and experience. Nearly all of them referred to how major tragedies had been covered before and how, during the coverage on September 11, they drew on that shared professional knowledge, which was in accordance with scholar A. S. Janik's description of the way professional people generally handle ethical problems within their fields.

Based on our interviews we may conclude that the norms of journalism are constantly refined as shown in the Figure 5.2:

Figure 5.2

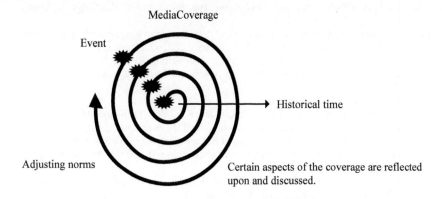

MediaCoverage

Event

Historical time

Adjusting norms

Certain aspects of the coverage are reflected upon and discussed.

Note: Development of professional norms. Every time journalists cover a major event they draw on previous experience and reflections. After the intense period of breaking news, aspects of the coverage are reflected upon by the individual journalist, discussed with other professionals and among the public. These reflections and discussions lead to increased awareness and adjusting of norms.

As is the case with other professional norms, the ten norms of crisis reporting described briefly in this chapter had developed through history of journalism, and many of our interviewees referred to previous troublesome or successful experiences with crises coverage.

When interviewed half a year after September 11, all of them were still reflecting on moral aspects of crises coverage, and most were prepared to do something different in the future even though overall they were proud of the coverage they provided in the days following the attacks.

The professionals mentioned historic examples of journalistic heroes, and the coverage on September 11 gave birth to new heroes whose behavior was described in normative stories that circulated within the professional community and that communicated the updated norms and values of crisis reporting.

Notes

1. Ross, A. (1968). *Directives and Norms* (pp. 83-84). London: Routledge & Kegan Paul.
2. Janik, A. S. (1994). Professional Ethics 'Applies' Nothing. In H. Pauer-Studer (Ed.): *Norms, Values and Society* (pp. 199), Vienna Circle Institute Yearbook: Kluwer Academic Publishers, Dordrecht.
3. Hansson, S. O. (2001). *The Structure of Values and Norms* (pp. 129), Cambridge: Cambridge University Press.
4. Ross, A. (1968). *Directives and Norms* (pp. 85). London: Routledge & Kegan Paul.
5. Ross, A. (1968). *Directives and Norms* (pp. 99). London: Routledge & Kegan Paul.
6. Pew Research Center (2001, September 19). American Psyche Reeling from Terror Attacks, press release Retrieved February 28, 2002, from *http://people-press. org/reports/display.php3?ReportID=3.*; WestGroup Research (September 24, 2001). Americans Believe Attack on America TV Coverage Accurate; Anchors Professional.
7. CNN transcripts 2001.
8. Greenberg, B. S., Hofschire, L., & Lachlan, K. (2002). Diffusion, Media Use and Interpersonal Communication Behaviors. In B. S. Greenberg (Ed.): *Communication and Terrorism. Public and Media Responses to 9/11* (pp. 3-16). New Jersey: Hampton Press; Pew Research Center (September 19, 2001). American Psyche Reeling from Terror Attacks.
9. WestGroup Research (September 24, 2001). Americans Believe Attack on America TV Coverage Accurate; Anchors Professional.
10. Hamilton, J. M., & Krimsky, G. A. (1996). *Hold the Press: The Inside Story on Newspapers.* Baton Rouge, LA: Louisiana State University Press.; Day, L. A. (2002). *Ethics in Media Communications—Cases & Controversies.* Los Angeles, CA: Thomson/Wadsworth; Merrill, J. C. (1997). *Journalism Ethics: Philosophical Foundations for News Media*, New York: St. Martin's Press.
11. Mogensen, K. (2007). How U.S. TV Journalists Talk About Objectivity in 9-11 Coverage. In T. Pludowski (Ed.): *How the World's News Media Reacted to 9/11: Essays from around the Globe* (pp. 301-318), Spokane, WA: Marquette Books.
12. Baraka, A. (2001). Somebody Blew Up America. Retrieved on March 23, 2007, from *http://www.amiribaraka.com/blew.html/*; Wikipedia (2007). Amiri Baraka. Retrieved on March 23, 2007, from *http://en.wikipedia.org/wiki/Amiri_Baraka*; Easterbrook, G. (November 5, 2001). Free Speech Doesn't Come without Cost, *The Wall Street Journal*, Pg. A1. McNair, B. (2007). UK Media Coverage of September 11. In T. Pludowski (Ed.): *How the World's News Media Reacted to 9/11: Essays from around the Globe* (pp. 32-33), Spokane, WA: Marquette Books LLG.
13. Johnson, T., & Kaye, B. (2004). Wag the Blog: How Reliance on Traditional Media and the Internet Influence Credibility Perceptions of Weblogs Among Blog Users, *Journalism & Mass Communication Quarterly*, 81(3), Pg. 622-642.; Seipp C. (2002). Online Uprising, *American Journalism Review*, 24(5), Pg. 42.
14. Commission on Freedom of the Press (1946) *A Free and Responsible Press.* Chicago, Illinois: The University of Chicago Press, Pg. 23-25.
15. Gasser, H. P. (2002). Acts of Terror, 'Terrorism' and International Humanitarian Law, IRRC, 84, Pg. 547-570.
16. *Broadcasting & Cable* (September 17, 2001). New York: Reed Business Information.
17. Shoemaker, P. J., & Reese, S. D. (1991). *Mediating the Message: Theories of Influences on Mass Media Content* (pg. 25). New York: Longman.

18. Society of Professional Journalists (2007). Society of Professional Journalists Code of Ethics. Retrieved on July 15, 2007, from *http://www.spj.org/ethicscode.asp*.
19. Mogensen, K., Lindsay, L., Li, X., Perkins, J., & Beardsley, M. (2002). How TV News Covered the Crisis: The Content of CNN, CBS, ABC, NBC, and Fox. In B.S. Greenberg (Ed.): *Communication and Terrorism: Public and Media Responses to 9/11 (*pg. 101-120). Cresskill, NJ: Hampton Press.

6

Sources: No Time for the Rolodex*

Sonora Jha and Ralph Izard

Any capable journalist knows that a news story is only as good as its sources. As a result, they often swear by—and at—their rolodex. Scholars as well have learned that journalistic sources are the key to scholarly studies of balance and bias. As a result, they too swear by—and at—the journalists' rolodex.

But what happens when there's no time for the rolodex? When no one can be reached? When those who can be reached have no time to talk? When those who have time to talk either don't know or have nothing newsworthy to say?

Broadcast coverage of 9/11 provided insight into those questions. The stories of that fateful day spanned issues of politics, pain, crime, economics, cultural collisions, heroism, foreign policy, large-scale destruction and personal devastation. No journalist had a rolodex that could encompass the story. Confusion was rampant. As the pictures unfolded, to whom did journalists turn for the words?

This tragedy occurred in two of the most multicultural cities in the country. Especially given the massive degree of public involvement, it is reasonable to look at how well journalists did in representing gender and race—indeed, the total community—in their choices of sources during this time of chaos and crisis. The question: Were journalists able to remain balanced and unbiased in the way they chose sources during a major emergency when careful planning was impossible?

---

* A version of this article was first published in the *Seattle Journal for Social Justice,* Vol. 4, Issue 1 (Fall Winter 2005).

Some researchers lay the blame for biased and skewed sourcing and other reporting inadequacies on the exigencies of live reporting.[1] Such reporting, they say, might actually thwart cohesive, thoughtful, ethical newsgathering and reporting processes. Clearly, September 11, 2001, provided a classic example of this problem.

Research indicates that the media communicate long-standing cultural presumptions without consciously and consistently promoting a particular racial mindset.[2] The news, therefore, reflects a sort of journalistic "common sense" in relation to relying on sources for information. If journalists think about it, they should know their own cultural values and sensibilities might determine whom they use as sources in their stories.[3]

The result, then, is that certain psychological processes may lead to inadvertent bias.[4] Robert M. Entman, in 1990, referred to this unconscious stereotyping of minorities as "modern racism."[5] He found that when blacks were the subject of the lead in local news stories, 75 percent of the stories dealt with violent crime. Blacks also were portrayed as more dangerous than whites.

The same problem applies to Latinos, the largest minority group in the United States, who appear very infrequently as prime-time characters on network television. Even then, they are more likely to appear in sitcoms than on network news.

Activists and scholars on diversity issues in the media argue that diversity is achieved not by just ensuring adequate representation in numbers but by making the representation more *inclusive*.[6] This means that African-Americans, for example, should not be used as sources only in stories about their community or "black issues." They should be used routinely as sources in all stories.

At least one study[7] has found that in the months after 9/11, not surprisingly under the circumstances, Arab-Americans were sought out as sources more than African-Americans. The study concluded that some racial minorities today might have to "compete" with other minorities for representation in news coverage.

Competition for space in news coverage traditionally has had a gender component as well as a racial component. But research results with regard to the race and sex of correspondents on network newscasts, topics of the stories they cover, and the roles of newsmakers presented in the news is not encouraging. Little change is noted, even in the face of an increase in demographics of minorities in the general population by the twenty-first century.

Studies have shown over the past two decades that women are not only diminished as news sources, but, even when they are used, are unlikely to be approached in a professional capacity, no matter what the gender of the reporter or the topic of the story.[8] On the other hand, a remarkable number of reporters covering the disaster of 9/11 at ground zero were women.[9] This makes it possible to ask another question: When women journalists are in the midst of a story that is making world news, involves terror, tragedy and politics, to whom do they reach out as sources of news?

This study looked at the first twenty-four hours of "live" breaking news coverage by CNN, CBS, and NBC to see whether journalists who normally would be cognizant of diversity in their coverage manage to maintain that attitude when they had no time to plan.

Of specific interest was whether news networks cited sources of one racial/ethnic category or one gender more than the other. Examination also was conducted of the type of sources used (official/authoritative versus non-official/non-authoritative) and race or gender of the sources to see if any relationships emerged. The study also focused on whether a relationship existed between the race and gender of the reporter or the race/gender of the sources they cited.

The coding resulted in a count of a total of 2,219 speakers/ voices, of which 778 were on CBS, 343 were on CNN and 1,098 were on NBC. Of the total number of speakers/voices, 1,983 appeared in coverage of the events in New York City and 236 in coverage of the plane crashing into the Pentagon. Excluding anchors and reporters, the total number of sources was 1,829.

White Males Dominate the Coverage

The analysis found that 66.26 percent of the sources (1,212 of the 1,829 total) were male, and 13.66 percent of the sources (250 of the 1,829) were female. The gender of 20.06 percent (367 of the 1,829) could not be determined for various reasons, including the use of unidentified sources by journalists.

Whites were predominantly used as sources. Of the 1,829 sources, 60.41 percent (1,105) were white, and 3.55 percent (65) were African-American. Four sources were identified as Hispanic (0.21 percent) and 92 sources (5.03 percent) were identified as "Other." The race or ethnicity of 563, or 30.78 percent, of the sources could not be determined.

A significant difference existed between the number of white and non-white sources in each category of source importance. Reporters showed a distinct preference in the "named officials" category for white sources, quoting 413 whites and only 16 African-Americans, one Hispanic and 39 who were categorized as "other." In 120 cases, race/ethnicity was unknown.

The pattern repeated itself in the "authoritative" category, with 259 white sources, 14 African-Americans, one Hispanic, 13 "other" and 80 cases of "unknown" race/ethnicity. The same pattern showed up in the case of "non-authoritative" sources, of whom 358 were white, 28 were African American, one was Hispanic, 12 were "other," and 107 were "unknown."

In addition, 45 of the unnamed officials were white, five were African-American, one was Hispanic, seven belonged to "other" race/ethnicities. Race or ethnicity in 232 cases in which unnamed officials were cited could not be determined.

Similar patterns were evident with gender. A clear, significant division along gender lines was seen in regard to the type of source used. In the "named official" category, 481 sources were male, 21 were female, and 87 were cases in which the gender was "unknown", i.e., not mentioned in the coverage. When it came to authoritative sources, 297 were male, 31 were female, and 39 were "unknown." The only source category in which females were cited in larger numbers was that of the "non-authoritative" source—301 were males, 178 were female,, and 27 were unknown. When officials were unnamed, 90 were male, 17 were female, and 183 could not be determined.

It became immediately clear that no matter what the race of the reporter, an across-the-board preference emerged for white sources over non-whites.

Reporters' Gender Has Little Impact on Source Selection

In addition, the gender of the reporters seemed to have little impact on the gender of those they approached as sources. Little difference existed between source choices by male or female reporters, but, once again, the scales were tilted heavily in favor of male sources.

In conclusion, the findings present a perhaps understandable, but nevertheless disturbing, picture of source bias during crisis news coverage, with a strong tendency among journalists to veer toward the traditional authority figure of the "white male official."

The study shows an overwhelming reliance on "white" sources and a poor (almost absent) representation of African-Americans and Hispanics, in particular, for all three networks examined.

The near absence of female sources in every category of source used except the "non-authoritative" source would suggest that 9/11 was a "male" story with little impact on women and little participation by them. Moreover, even though female sources rose somewhat in number as non-authoritative sources, no such rise was seen for non-whites as "non-authoritative sources."

These two findings indicate what perhaps is an unconscious discrimination on the part of reporters, no doubt intensified during reportage of an unprecedented crisis. The nature of the story/coverage does not appear to be responsible for this bias in favor of white or male sources—the 9/11 tragedy was not merely a political/business/foreign policy story, for which it might be argued by some that most sources tend to be white and male.

The findings also indicate that diversification in the newsroom by race, ethnicity, and gender seems to have had little impact on gender and race bias in news coverage.

Sourcing under Extreme Journalistic Pressure

It is not the intention of this study to criticize journalists who were under perhaps unbearable pressure in the early hours of one of the most chaotic events in this nation's history. They did their jobs and did them well in describing a situation that could not be described. They provided meaningful information, they served their audiences, they captured the human loss as well as the property loss, and they helped lead the nation to as much healing as the circumstances would allow.

It is perhaps true that journalists in the face of catastrophe do not have time to think. They call upon their experience and their knowledge to prompt instinctive reaction. Nevertheless, fairness and balance remain journalistic virtues. African-Americans, Hispanics, other minorities, and women suffered as well during 9/11. It was their story just as much as it was the story of white males. They deserved more intention. They deserved to be included.

A study by Xigen Li and Ralph Izard indicates that 34 percent of newspaper sources and nearly 11 percent of network television sources in the early hours of 9/11 were witnesses to the disaster. In addition, 23 percent of the newspaper sources and 4 percent of the television sources were defined as experts.[10] It seems logical to assume the possibility that greater racial, ethnic, and gender diversity was possible among these people.

Perhaps the central lesson evolving from this study is the need for change in the journalistic mindset. Even when the rolodex doesn't work, automatic responses during crisis should be based on a broader perspective. The importance of covering the total community, not just the white male portion of it, must become a part of that journalistic instinct, not just something well-intentioned people do when they have time to plan.

Notes

1. Cleland, G. L., & Ostroff, D. H. (1988). Satellite News Gathering and News Department Operations, *Journalism Quarterly*, 65, pg. 946-951; Dunsmore, B. (1996). *The Next War: Live?* Cambridge: Harvard University Press; Murrie, M. (1998). Communication Technology and the Correspondent. In J. S. Foote (Ed.): *Live from the Trenches* (pg. 94-104). Carbondale, IL: Southern Illinois University Press; Seib, P. (2000). *Going Live: Getting the News Right in a Real-Time, Online World*, Lanham, MD: Rowman & Littlefield; Tuggle, C. A. & Huffman, S. (2001). Live Reporting in Television News: Breaking News or Black Holes?, Journal of Broadcasting & Electronic Media, 45(2), pg. 335-344.
2. Entman, R. M., & Rojecki, A. (2000). *The Black Image in the White Mind.* Chicago: University of Chicago Press.
3. Campbell, C. P. (1995). *Race, Myth, and the News.* Thousand Oaks, CA: Sage.
4. Coleman, R. (2003). Race and Ethical Reasoning: The Importance of Race to Journalistic Decision Making, *Journalism & Mass Communication Quarterly*, 80(2), pg. 295-310; Stocking, H. S. & Gross, P. H. (1989). *How Do journalists Think: A Proposal for the Study of Cognitive Bias in Newsmaking.* Bloomington, IN: Smith Research Center, Indiana University.
5. Entman, R. M. (1990). Modern Racism and the Images of Blacks in Local Television News, *Critical Studies in Mass Communication*, 7, pg. 332-345.
6. Woods, K. M. (2002, August 6). Handling race/ethnicity in descriptions, *Poynter Online*. Retrieved on April 13, 2008, from *https://www.poynter.org/content/content_view.asp?id=9518.*
7. Domke, D., Garland, P., Billeaubeaux, A., & Hutcheson, J. (2003). Insights into U.S. Racial Hierarchy: Racial Profiling, News Sources, and September 11, *Journal of Communication*, 5, pg. 606-623.
8. Whitney, C., Fritzler, M., Jones, S., Mazzarella, S. & Rakow, L. (1989). Geographic and Source Biases in Network Television News, 1982-1984, *Journal of Broadcasting & Electronic Media*, 33(2), pg.159-174; Liebler, C. & Smith, S. (1997). Tracking Gender Differences: A Comparative Analysis of Network Correspondents and their Sources, *Journal of Broadcasting & Electronic Media*, 41 (1), pg. 58-61.
9. Sylvester, J. & Huffman, S. (2002). *Women Journalists at Ground Zero: Covering Crisis.* Lanham, MD.: Rowman & Littlefield.
10. Li, X. and Izard, R. (2005). 9/11 TV, Newspapers Coverage Reveals Similarities, Differences. In E.K. Grusin, & S.H. Utt (Ed.): *Media in an American Crisis: Studies of September 11, 2001* (pp. 89-103). New York: University Press of America, Inc.

7

Crisis Interviewing:
Preparation and Sensitivity

Ralph Izard

When American Airlines Flight 77, in the hands of terrorists, crashed into The Pentagon on September 11, 2001, among those whose lives were forever changed were Rosemary Dillard and Abraham Scott. Both lost spouses on that tragic day.

Dillard's husband, Eddie, 54, was a passenger on Flight 77. Scott's wife, Janice, 46, worked at the Pentagon in the Office of the Administrative Secretary of the Army.

In addition to their personal losses, Dillard and Scott subsequently were thrown into a glare of public attention they never before had experienced. Both became journalistic subjects as a result of their losses; both dealt with journalists after becoming active members of a committee that represented family members. And, of course, both were involved in the Washington Post's project of presenting a story about each victim.

They had to relinquish part of their private lives. They had to answer questions. It was only partly a choice they made. They had to do it. And, in spite of their inexperience, they learned about reporters and journalistic demands. Dillard and Scott came away from these experiences with mixed feelings. Their experiences ranged from dealing with sensitive, respectful, and thoughtful journalists to some who were overly demanding and downright insensitive.

In general, Dillard and Scott were in strong agreement that:

- Sources for coverage of the September 11 tragedy were predominantly Caucasians, especially those in official positions. This was partly circumstance, but it also resulted from what appeared to be conscious choices by journalists.
- While they had the usual problems with what they believed to be statements taken out of context and with being misquoted, their most heart-felt criticism was the belief that many journalists were ill-prepared, and sometimes insensitive, at the time of the interviews.
- They found their treatment to be mostly fair and reasonable in one-on-one conversations with journalists, but experienced group interviews that were much less satisfactory.
- Their experience indicated to them that African American journalists seem to overcompensate toward whites when given the choice.
- They recognized that journalists do face particular problems in seeking source diversity—for example, the fact that Caucasians are larger in number, and African Americans often are reticent about sharing their private lives.

Perhaps equally important, however, "It's just easier for white folks to talk to white folks, I guess," Dillard said as she tried to sum up what she perceived to be problems of media coverage of the tragic incident in her city of about 60 percent African-American population. "So there were a lot of disparities. In the coverage, in the treatment, just in everything."

For example, Dillard remembered the occasion on which she was the principal organizer of a remembrance walk for the victims, and "most of the journalists that were there went to all of the white folks; they did not come to me.... (Y)ou could see at that walk when it came on TV, they showed only Caucasians, and there were several black journalists (there)."

Scott sought to put the situation into a broader perspective:

> I may be talking apples and oranges, but throughout this process you could identify discrimination in terms of not only the color barrier, but also military versus non-military, contractor versus military, the airline versus the military. And just to give you an example, the Navy (appeared more likely) in terms of being given information, being invited to certain things, being out in the forefront in terms of being interviewed by reporters.

This is not to say that Dillard and Scott had nothing but bad experiences with journalists. Of those journalists with whom they dealt, they found many to be sympathetic and understanding, at least when the situation involved a single journalist in a personal conversation.

"And I just want to point out that with the exception of maybe one, all of my interviews were done by black reporters," Scott said.

Dillard added: "Nine times out of ten it is really a very good job. It is rare that it's a one-on-one, but they have all been very thoughtful in the things that they ask and the way that they ask the questions. And their whole demeanor ... is just very thoughtful in the way that they ask the questions."

Given these gratifying experiences, Scott and Dillard did note some problems, even when dealing with black journalists.

"You know, I, in my infinite wisdom, look at it this way," Dillard said. "If you are a black journalist, and you go out and interview somebody black, then they are looking at you like, why do you just talk to blacks? You know, you get the stigma (of) 'all you talk to are African Americans.'"

Dillard also spoke of one group interview with which she was not pleased.

"She (the reporter) was horrible. There were six of us sitting in the room. She asked everybody the same question. By the time it got to the sixth person, they couldn't think of anything to say. Because everybody else had said everything. I called CNN and told them how I felt and what a poor job she did.... If she didn't want to interview us, she shouldn't have come. And she should have been prepared, and she was not. Some of these people had driven from a long distance to come over here to do this, and we were volunteering to do this, and that was the way we were treated by her."

She also mentioned another case, this involving the lack of common courtesy to another family member of a victim: "(ABC) was supposed to interview her, and so she went out and got a new outfit, bought flowers for her house, had it all spruced up, and they never showed."

Scott said his worst interview was with a non-African-American journalist who "wasn't prepared, I don't think. Because he was feeling for questions, whereas the other gentlemen and ladies were very spontaneous and thoughtful."

Scott and Dillard, however, did recognize that journalists who consciously seek source diversity often face obstacles in what they perceived to be reluctance on the part of some sources.

"Telling the story is hard, and when you tell the story over and over, it does get harder because it's like it is never going to go to bed," Dillard said. "It is never going to end, and you'd like at the end of the day to be able to say: 'Job well done; it is over.'"

Furthermore, she said, reporters need to understand that many African Americans who were affected won't speak out.

"They won't participate, so it is not just the journalists. I think we are raised more (to believe) that if you have a problem in your house, it stays in your house. Because ... we were raised (to believe) that you just don't tell your family business. So we are not going to come out there and be on TV or say anything, and consequently we get left out."

Scott added his belief that among factors that cause disparity between Caucasians and African-Americans, especially at The Pentagon, are differences in personal backgrounds.

"The Caucasians have been exposed to the world, like the military, and they are more apt to speak out as opposed to a lot of the African-Americans who were born and raised in this area." Many African Americans, therefore, lack confidence to speak to a reporter, "and a lot of them think that's one of the reasons why there were more interviews conducted of Caucasians than African Americans."

In spite of these factors, they said, it is the role of journalism to seek out sources consciously, to speak to everyone and to deal with all people in a respectful manner that helps make them comfortable when they tell their part of the story.

When Dillard and Scott responded to a request to give advice to journalists—especially journalists dealing with a fast-moving crisis story—they responded like the latest textbook on diversity.

"To seek out everybody," Dillard said. "Not to dwell on the rich and the powerful and the famous or just the Caucasians. Because if you notice even the Caucasians who were interviewed were not poor Caucasians. They were all very affluent; they were captains; they were commanders. Journalists didn't go to just a private; they didn't go that low."

To journalistic managers who make assignments, the pair strongly urged assurance that the assigned reporters "are qualified and, in their qualifications, they need to either be in your race or having had some experience with your race." In other words, they need to be prepared.

And, finally, Scott presented a plea from his experience of losing a wife in one of the nation's greatest tragedies: "I would tell them that they need to be sensitive to the needs of the family members."

8

Television Impact: More Than Words Alone[*]

Renita Coleman and H. Denis Wu

While one can argue forever about the concept of journalistic objectivity, some news stories are so packed with emotion that it is extremely difficult for reporters and editors to remain strictly neutral. Such was the case with 9/11 (and a few years later, in fact, with hurricanes Katrina and Rita). While journalists are taught detachment, it may not always be possible and, arguably perhaps, sharing the emotion being felt by the public may even strengthen the impact of news coverage.

This is particularly true of television journalism, often done at the time and at the scene where the emotional impact is greatest. Broadcast journalists most frequently try to carefully structure what they say. But words alone cannot possibly characterize television, the ultimate visual medium. Unlike print, viewers experience time and space with the journalists on the screen. And, for that reason, facial gestures and body language convey messages that can reinforce the intent of the spoken word—or they can negate the spoken message entirely.

Such nonverbal communication of broadcasters is particularly important because of the effects it can have on viewers. Journalists' projections of anger, fear or stress may induce the same emotions in viewers,[1] and public perceptions of bias in reporting—even if in facial expression—may directly impact the believability of that reporting, in short, may impact media credibility.[2]

[*]A previous version of this article was published in *Journal of Broadcasting & Electronic Media*, Vol. 50, No. 1, 2006, pp. 1-17.

Television was Americans' main source of information on September 11, 2001.[3] Viewers watched an average of eight hours of television a day on 9/11, with 18 percent viewing upwards of 13 hours that day, and scholars have found a link between increased viewing and increased stress.[4]

Thus, this study has import for broadcasters seeking to be seen as credible news conveyors, and 9/11 is not the only circumstance in which this knowledge is useful. Terrorist acts are becoming more frequent, as can be seen in the cases of Oklahoma City, Waco, the Madrid train bombings and the Russian school massacre.

Broadcasters also may be overcome with emotion while covering news such as school shootings, hostage standoffs, hurricanes, tornadoes, high-speed chases, out-of-control fires, and even trials that feature graphic images. Emotional testimony from victims' relatives can move reporters to emotional displays. The lessons learned from 9/11, as extreme as it was, may indeed be generalized to numerous other circumstances in which reporters find themselves, from wars to gruesome car accidents.

Nonverbal Communication Has Impact

The nonverbal component of communication is at least as important as the verbal content.[5] When verbal and nonverbal messages are contradictory, receivers typically believe the nonverbal message.[6] On television, especially, "expressions usually dominate words."[7] Verbal communication is more persuasive when factual arguments are presented, but nonverbal communication is more relevant to impression formation and emotional expression.[8] After all, effective communication involves both content and affect.[9]

While expressions may be masked with facial management techniques,[10] or overridden by suppressing or counterfeiting them,[11] few journalists are trained in these techniques.

The fact that broadcast journalists *are* instructed to be objective in their display of emotion, attitudes, and bias gives credence to how they present the information as well as what information they present.

This study does not intend to criticize journalists who covered the September 11, 2001, attacks, often at great personal risk. They did an exceptional job under unprecedented pressures. But journalists are human, and nonverbal displays may be difficult to control, even for trained professionals.

And, make no mistake about it. The journalists who covered 9/11 shared in the nation's intense emotion of the day. Those interviewed all admitted feeling the same emotions that viewers felt—fear, concern, anger. But they also said the pressure of covering the event kept them so busy that they could not focus on their feelings.

"We didn't get to experience what the rest of America got to experience, to just sit and watch this unfold and to experience our feelings and to remember our feelings. We're working the story," said Lester Holt, an anchor for MSNBC. "You are always one step ahead, and you can't absorb the enormity of what's happening on a human level. You know, I didn't have a chance to shed a tear like so many people did, to feel the grief and the shock and all of that because you just can't—there is not time."

The coverage of 9/11 was much more difficult for the New York-based networks than most national disaster stories. This was happening to them, in their city, to their friends and neighbors, to their country.

"Other breaking news stories—the Columbine School shooting, the Oklahoma City bombing or a plane crash or you name it, breaking news—didn't seem to affect us personally the way this did," said Marcy McGinnis, senior vice president for news coverage at CBS. "It was all sort of impersonal. But this story was very personal…. It happened in our city, so therefore it was something that affected you personally, but there was a point at which—and I say it was the point at which the Pentagon got hit—that it affected us as human beings, as American citizens as well as journalists."

Despite the pressures of the job and the broadcast canon to stay cool under fire, emotional outbreaks did occur in the newsrooms.

Sharri Berg, vice president of FOX News, said several people broke down under the emotion of the day. "(One of her news managers) was just looking up at the monitors, and tears filled his eyes, and he just kind of broke down and for a moment. I wanted to say 'what's wrong? You are in your mode, your walls are up, you are covering a story.'

"That was happening throughout the day with different people, and it was hitting people at different times," she said.

The journalists also had to deal with their personal concerns for family members and friends.

"I was very concerned about people I knew. I knew that my brother-in-law was in the building next door, the American Express building. I knew that other people that I know might be down there and could have been hurt. And I was aware of that, but I just sort of pushed that to the back of my head," said Al Ortiz, executive producer and director, special events, at CBS.

MSNBC's Holt agreed.

"Everybody who was covering the story that day has a personal connection," he said. "Other people lost friends, other people, it was their neighborhood. It was very real. We are used to covering things—bombing in Afghanistan, earthquakes in California—it is never, it isn't necessarily, someone you know. But you know this one shattered everybody's collective sense of security."

Nonverbal Expressions in the News

The presence of such an emotional atmosphere and the importance of how journalists deal with that emotion, therefore, prompted this study of news coverage of 9/11 from a nonverbal standpoint. Analysis was conducted of four networks (ABC, CBS, NBC and CNN) to look at whether broadcasters showed significant positive or negative nonverbal behavior.

The question? How successful were professionally trained broadcasters in controlling their nonverbal communication during the most traumatic and emotional event in recent memory? And, since previous research has documented that women convey emotion better than men,[12] and since at least 33 percent of broadcast journalists are female,[13] this study also explored whether female broadcasters would exhibit more nonverbal expressions than males. Also of interest was whether emotion varied according to the time of the day, i.e., whether journalists were more likely to show emotion early or later in the coverage of 9/11, and whether networks differed in broadcasters' total nonverbal expressions.

This study included 2,067 shots taken in the first twenty-four hours of newscasts about 9/11. CNN contributed about 30 percent of the total, ABC 26 percent, CBS 22 percent, and NBC 22 percent. As a result, the nonverbal expressions of 653 journalists were coded. The study measured six nonverbal dimensions that had been tested in previous studies: eyebrows, mouth and lips, head, overall face, overall body, and overall gesturing.[14] Of all the nonverbal cues, facial expressions carry the most information.[15] They are rich sources of direct and inferred information because they readily reveal mental states.[16]

Such was the focus of this study, and it confirmed the expectation that broadcasters would communicate significantly more nonverbal expressions (positive and negative combined) than neutral expressions during the first twenty-four hours of 9/11. Of the 653 journalists, 600 exhibited at least one non-neutral nonverbal expression during the first twenty-four hours.

A Gender Effect?

On the other hand, the study did not determine that female broadcasters would exhibit significantly more total nonverbal expressions than male broadcasters. Contrary to predictions of prior research, no significant difference between male and female broadcasters during the coverage of 9/11 was indicated.

While broadcasters overall may not have been entirely successful in concealing their nonverbal expressions, men and women had about the same rate of success (or failure) in this regard. This finding should help put to rest any lingering concerns over women being able to report as well as men on certain stories.

It is not possible to say from this correlational study whether women broadcasters learn to conceal their emotions or whether women who go into broadcasting already have this trait.[17] But it is encouraging that, for once, no gender difference was found when other indications say it should be there.

Time of Day

Significant differences were found, however, in emotion shown at different times of that terrible day. The highest average of nonverbal expressions came in the second eight-hour period, from 5 p.m. Sept. 11 to 1 a.m. the next day. The lowest average occurred in the final eight-hour segment, from 1 a.m. to 9 a.m. on Sept. 12. On the negative side, reporters made the most negative nonverbal expressions during the first period (46 percent), immediately followed by the second period (44 percent).

That the second eight hours produced the highest averages for emotion is surprising at first glance; one might intuitively expect the early hours of the event to produce more emotion.

However, only after the event had unfolded and no more incidents occurred did journalists begin to contemplate the implications of such a massive, planned undertaking. In this second period, they lost their professional neutrality and were more likely to visually express emotions. And, as described in Chapter 2, coverage by CNN during this stage consisted partly of a press conference and a "Larry King Live" talk show in which people were asked to describe how they helped one another.

Differences among Networks

Significant differences did exist among networks, and this agrees with other research on bias in political coverage.[18]

Of the four networks examined (CNN, ABC, NBC, and CBS), CNN had the fewest nonverbal expressions, while NBC yielded the highest average, and the difference was significant. Furthermore, significant differences occurred among the networks in the valence of broadcasters' nonverbal expressions. ABC and NBC, for example, were statistically different in the degree of nonverbal expressions. NBC's coverage was the most negative, followed by CBS, CNN, and ABC.

Given the enormity of the tragedy, it may not be too surprising that journalists' underlying attitudes and emotions were revealed nonverbally, or that the nonverbal information they conveyed was overwhelmingly negative. Yet, broadcast journalists would be surprised at this finding. They believe they are more successful at adhering to the journalistic tenet of impartiality. This was not upheld – at least not in nonverbal communication.

Nonverbal Communications and Objectivity

This study aimed to extend the findings on broadcasters' nonverbal communication from one arena—political coverage—to another, that of breaking news. That broadcasters do exhibit nonverbal behavior in at least two different settings makes it less likely that the content of the story is the only explanation. That seasoned network anchors and report-ers were so frequently unable to convey neutral nonverbal expressions is worth noting.

These findings may give ammunition to critics of journalism who say journalists are not objective—at least not in the nonverbal content of their messages. In this content analysis, the nonverbal behaviors of broadcasters covering the first twenty-four hours of 9/11 more often conveyed positive or negative expressions than neutral expressions. The goal of objectivity in news coverage is deeply entrenched in journalistic culture, but research makes it clear that journalists routinely do not achieve that goal, at least nonverbally and with such a tragic occurrence. This is particularly the case given current television emphases on talk shows that feature opinions.

This would indicate that training in facial management techniques may be appropriate for broadcasters. Journalists need to develop emotion-ally neutral ways of interpreting the events with which they deal.[19] It is especially important to journalists in the second stage of crisis because an important element of this stage is that the media try to ease tensions among the audience and increase national morale. If their nonverbal behavior does not convey this message, it is unlikely their words will have the intended effect.

On the other hand, it may not be so clear because in this context, it may be the case that such opinions even facilitate the easing of tensions. In fact, some of the journalists interviewed said the showing of emotion on 9/11 did not detract from the coverage; rather, they saw it as needed and a positive force of their reaching out to their publics.

"There is a time that I think it is OK to be human," MSNBC's Holt said. "This was a story that didn't have two sides to it. You didn't have to worry about being impartial. So it was OK to be factual, but at the same time it was OK to show some emotion. I think sometimes we get out of journalism school, we are like 'I am a journalist and I am not affected by anything.' Well, you know what, you are also a human being, and you were affected."

So, the debate continues. But beyond the implications for whether objectivity is an impossible goal for journalism—or whether, indeed, it is only circumstantially desirable, the results of this study do raise questions about what effects these biased nonverbal expressions of broadcasters have on viewers.

It's important that journalists understand the potential impact of their nonverbal behavior and whether their choices are conscious or unconscious. No matter how well hidden, journalists' nonverbal behavior can stir viewers' emotions, influence the opinions they form and even affect their attitudes and behavior. Any journalistic technique loses its impact when overdone or when done without understanding of what it means. Inevitably, this will have an effect on credibility.

Notes

1. Englis, B.G. (1994). The Role of Affect in Political Advertising: Voter Emotional Responses to the Nonverbal Behavior of Politicians. In M. C. Eddie, T. C. Brock, & D.W. Stewart (Eds.): *Attention, Attitude and Affect in Response to Advertising* (pg. 223-247). Hillsdale, NJ: Lawrence Erlbaum.
2. American Society of Newspaper Editors (1999). *Examining Our Credibility: Perspectives of the Public and the Press*. Reston, VA: ASNE.
3. Robertson, L. (2001). Anchoring the Nation, *American Journalism Review*, 23, pg. 40-45.
4. Schuster, M. A. (2001). A National Survey of Stress Reactions After the September 11, 2001 Terrorist Attacks, *New England Journal of Medicine*, 345(20), pg. 1507-1512.
5. Argyle, M., Alkema, F., & Gilmour, R. (1971). The Communication of Friendly and Hostile Attitudes by Verbal and Nonverbal Signals, *European Journal of Social Psychology*, 1, pg. 385-402; Graber, D. (1990). Seeing in Remembering: How Visuals Contribute to Learning From Television News, *Journal of Communication*, 40(3), pg. 134-155.

6. Richmond, V.P., McCroskey, J.C., & Payne, S.K. (1991). *Nonverbal Behavior in Interpersonal Interactions.* Englewood Cliffs, NJ: Prentice-Hall.
7. Meyrowitz, J. (1985). *No Sense of Place: The Impact of Electronic Media on Social Behavior* (p. 103). New York: Oxford University Press.
8. Burgoon, J. K., Birk, T., & Pfau, M. (1990). Nonverbal Behaviors, Persuasion, and Credibility. *Human Communication Research*, 17, (1), Pg. 140-169.
9. Pfau, M. (1990). A Channel Approach to Television Influence, *Journal of Broadcasting and Electronic Media*, 34, 2, Pg. 195-214.
10. Ekman, P., & Friesen, W.V. (1975). *Unmasking the Face.* Englewood Cliffs, NJ: Prentice-Hall; DePaulo, B. M. (1992). Nonverbal Behavior and Self-Presentation, *Psychological Bulletin*, 111(2), pg. 203-243.
11. Buck, R., & VanLear, C.A. (2002). Verbal and Nonverbal Communication: Distinguishing Symbolic, Spontaneous, and Pseudo-Spontaneous Nonverbal Behavior, *Journal of Communication*, 52(3), pg. 522-541.
12. For a review, see Hall, J.A. (1984). *Nonverbal Sex differences: Communication Accuracy and Expressive Style.* Baltimore, MD/London, England: Johns Hopkins University Press; Wagner, H.L., Buck, R., & Winterbotham, M. (1993). Communication of Specific Emotions: Gender Differences in Sending Accuracy and Communication Measures, *Journal of Nonverbal Behavior*, 17(1), pg. 29-54.
13. Weaver, D., Beam, R., Brownlee, B., Voakes, P., & Wilhoit, G.C. (2007). *The American Journalist in the 21st Century.* Mahwah, NJ: Lawrence Erlbaum.
14. Mullen, L. (1998). Close-Ups of the President: Photojournalistic Distance from 1945 to 1974, *Visual Communication Quarterly*, Spring, pg. 4-6; Moriarty, S. E., & Garramone, G. M. (1986). A Study of Newsmagazine Photographs of the 1984 Presidential Campaign, *Journalism Quarterly*, 63, pg. 728-734; Moriarty, S. E., & Popovich, M. N. (1991). Newsmagazine Visuals and the 1988 Presidential Election, *Journalism Quarterly*, 68(3), pg. 371-380; Sullivan, D. G. & Masters, R. D. (1988). "Happy warriors": Leaders' Facial Displays, Viewers' Emotions, and Political Support, *American Journal of Political Science*, 32(2), pg. 345-368.
15. Mehrabian, A. (1968). Inference of Attitudes from the Posture, Orientation, and Distance of a Communicator, *Journal of Consulting and Clinical Psychology*, 32, pg. 296-308.
16. Ekman, P. (Ed.) (1983). *Emotion in the Human Face* (2nd ed.). New York: Cambridge University Press.
17. DePaulo, B.M. (1992). Nonverbal Behavior and Self-Presentation, *Psychological Bulletin*, 111(2), pg. 203-208; See, for example, Nacos, B. (1994). *Terrorism and the Media: From the Iran Hostage Crisis to the Oklahoma City Bombing.* New York: Columbia University Press; Chiasson Jr., L (1995) (Ed.). *The Press in Times of Crisis.* Westport, CN: Praeger; Caldwell, J.T. (1995). *Televisuality, Style, Crisis and Authority in American Television.* New Brunswick, NJ: Rutgers University Press; Altheide, D.L. (2002). *Creating Fear: News and the Construction of Crisis.* New York: Aldine de Gruyter. Nimmo, D., & Combs, J. E. (1985). *Nightly Horrors: Crises Coverage in Television Network News.* Knoxville, TN: The University of Tennessee Press. Graber, D. A. (1980). *Mass Media and American Politics* (pp. 225-241). Washington, DC: *Congressional Quarterly Press.* See, for example, Johnson, T. J., & Boudreau, T. (1996). Turning the Spotlight Inward: How Five Leading News Organizations Covered the Media in the 1992 Presidential Election, *Journalism & Mass Communication Quarterly*, 73 (3), pg. 657-671; Delli Carpini, M. X., & Williams, B. A. (1984). Terrorism and the media: Patterns of occurrence and presentation, 1969-1980. In H. H. Han (Ed.): *Terrorism, Political Violence, and World Order* (pp. 103-134). New York: University Press of America; Semetko, H. A., & Valkenburg, P.M. (2000). Framing European Politics: A Content Analysis of

Press and Television News, *Journal of Communication*, 50 (2), pg. 93-109. Included in this study were five television networks (ABC, CBS, NBC, CNN, and FOX News) and eight national newspapers (The *New York Times, Washington Post, Los Angeles Times, Milwaukee Journal Sentinel, Denver Post, St. Louis Post-Dispatch, Houston Chronicle,* and *Atlanta Journal and Constitution*). Editorial (September 5, 2002). Death, Destruction, Charity, Salvation, War, Money, Real Estate, Spouses, Babies, and Other September 11 Statistics, *New York Magazine.* Retrieved on March 31, 2008, from *http://nymag.com/news/articles/wtc/1year/numbers.htm.*

18. Friedman, H. S., Mertz, T. I., & DiMatteo, M. R. (1980). Perceived Bias in the Facial Expressions of Television News Broadcasters, *Journal of Communication,* 30, pg. 103-111.

19. Duckworth, D. H. (1991). Facilitating Recovery from Disaster-Work Experiences, *British Journal of Guidance & Counselling,* 19 (1), pg.13-22.

9

Radio's Role: First You Go into High Gear, and Then You Cry

Judith Sylvester and Suzanne Huffman

As throngs of survivors made their uncertain way out of lower Manhattan to escape the death and destruction behind them on September 11, 2001, the importance of radio in a local story became immediately apparent. Radio distinguished itself as a way many learned of what had happened, what to expect, and what to do. This was made more complicated for local New York broadcasters because the attacks brought down the transmitter towers that served many of the city's media outlets.

This is the 9/11 story of WNYC, the local National Public Radio (NPR) affiliate whose staff members were among those journalists who risked their lives to get information to shell-shocked New Yorkers and to Americans everywhere. In spite of the loss of its transmitter, WNYC continuously supplied New Yorkers and NPR in Washington, DC, with first-hand information about the attacks and their effects. Americans across the country listened intently as NPR affiliates nationwide picked up the broadcasts of reporters Beth Fertig, Amy Eddings, and Kerry Nolan.

A Plane Has Hit the World Trade Center

September 11 was primary election day in New York. WNYC reporter Beth Fertig was sleeping late in her Greenwich Village apartment because she expected to be out most of the night covering the candidates. At 9 a.m. a frantic phone call from her acting news director, Kevin Beasley, woke her up. "A plane has crashed into the World Trade Center," he said. "You have to get here right away. I'm going to need you to find the mayor or the police commissioner."

"I was completely taken by surprise. I had no idea what he was talking about," Fertig said. "A few weeks earlier somebody had tried to parachute onto the Statue of Liberty, so I thought, 'Oh, it's just another crank who did something stupid and bumped into the World Trade Center.' I didn't know it was a real plane."

She turned on her radio and remembers hearing Mark Hilan, WNYC's morning anchor, saying a plane had struck the World Trade Center, and it was not clear what was going on. "But, I still wasn't paying attention to how serious it was," she said. "I thought, 'Okay, I'll go cover this little fire, and then I'll go cover the election.'" As she was preparing to leave her Greenwich Village apartment, she heard Hilan interviewing an eyewitness in the studio. "I remember thinking, 'That's really weird. I don't recognize that voice.'" She said the man turned out to be someone who had seen the attack from his window. Then she heard Hilan say he might have to leave the studio.

She ran downstairs and outside where she had a perfect view of the World Trade Center. "I saw all these people in the street, staring. I looked south, and the Twin Towers were clearly visible to me with holes in them and burning—these big, black holes in each tower and flames shooting out. It was a perfect, blue-sky day, and the towers were perfectly illuminated by the sun—sparkling, silver towers with these holes in them and with flames jumping out. It was the most striking image. I didn't think it was real. I was looking at it like a surrealist painting. Then I realized, 'Oh my God, this is *real*!' I could smell the smoke. Everybody's out in the street. It felt very weird."

With her bag of equipment, Fertig ran to her train station on Bleecker Street, approximately a mile and a half and three stops from WNYC's studio in the Municipal Building, near City Hall and six blocks from the Trade Center. When she arrived at her stop, the air was thick with smoke. She saw "little bits of stuff" floating around her, and she realized this was not a "little fire," and she was not going to vote.

She was, in fact, involved in a huge human tragedy.

"Everyone was crowding around City Hall. I ran up to our newsroom, and no one was there. The whole place had been evacuated except that Mark Hilan, host of *Morning Edition*, was on the air. And, a couple of our managers were there, and they were saying the building had been evacuated. So, I ran downstairs again, and there are a few people from work standing outside the building." The people she met were from programming, and none knew if any reporters had made it to the scene. None of their cell phones was working, and long lines were forming at the pay phones.

Since she was assigned to find the mayor or the police commissioner, she ran to Police Plaza, which was right behind WNYC's building. The building had been evacuated. No one was allowed in. At City Hall, she was told that the building also had been evacuated. The police told her the mayor had gone to the World Trade Center to his bunker, called the Emergency Command Center, in 7 World Trade Center, next to the Twin Towers.

"I'm thinking, 'He wouldn't be crazy enough to go to his bunker if the towers are burning, would he?' So, I run back across the street to my little cluster of people from work, and I saw the program director, Dean Cappello. I said, 'Dean, I'm just going to go. I don't know what's going on, but I'm just going to go.'" He told her not to do anything crazy.

WNYC Radio reporter Amy Eddings was assigned to cover Alan Hevesi, a Democratic candidate for mayor as he campaigned with the head of the New York teachers' union. She showed up for a scheduled campaign stop in Brooklyn Heights, near one of its busiest subway stations. With her heavy recording equipment, she was carrying a pair of her fiancé's shoes to take to a shoeshine shop near the World Trade Center. Her wedding to WNYC anchor Mark Hilan was scheduled for September 15.

"I was also carrying my cell phone and its charger," she said. "The battery was dead. I was planning on charging it up during the day in order to use it that night from Hevesi's election night headquarters."

Hevesi was late. He hopped out of his car and announced to everyone that a plane had hit the Trade Center. Eddings said her feeling was that it must have been a small prop plane, a little Cessna. She ruefully thought that someone else would have to cover it, since she was following Hevesi.

"Brooklyn Heights is a mostly residential neighborhood, right across the East River from Lower Manhattan, with a great view of the Twin Towers," she said. "Where I was, tall buildings obscured the view. But, suddenly over Hevesi's shoulder I could see a white cloud of debris forming on the sky. I pointed to it, and Hevesi and others muttered, 'Oh, my God!' This was a bigger story than I imagined."

Eddings' pager went off. It was her newsroom, asking her to go to the scene. She hopped onto the subway. "I was very lucky I got on before they shut the system down. I got to Fulton Street, about three or four blocks east of the World Trade Center. I started walking west toward the towers." She could sense panic. "People were running. There were loud voices."

She knew only about the first plane, but by the time she exited the subway the second plane had hit, and both towers were smoking. "I did not know what to expect. I didn't know what I was looking for. I steeled myself to see blood and guts. I didn't see anything like I thought I was going to see," she said.

People were clustered on the sidewalk and in the streets, watching the towers, but Eddings did not see scores of injured people. Lots of people were streaming out of the towers. Several were crying and visibly upset. She saw one man lying on the street, unconscious, with a gash on his forehead. Blood was running toward the gutter, and Eddings stepped over it. She asked the paramedics who were tending him if he had been hurt by falling debris. A bystander said, "No, it was by all the people!"

"I kept looking for big parts of the planes. Instead, I saw lots of shoes, nuts and bolts, headphones, a book bag...."

Kerry Nolan began the morning of September 11 as she did most weekday mornings, packing her son off to school and letting the dog out in the yard to run. As the local host for the weekend *All Things Considered* and *Weekend Edition Saturday and Sunday* for WNYC, she normally spends weekday mornings at her home in Atlantic Highlands, New Jersey, directly across the Sandy Hook Bay from the Twin Towers. Her son had just left the house when the phone rang.

The call was from a producer at the Canadian Broadcast Company (CBC) in Toronto for whom she had done some freelance work. "Are you watching CNN?" he asked. Nolan responded, "No. Should I be?" His answer was, "Well, you might want to put on the TV because you're going live to Canada in about five minutes." She turned on CNN to see the first tower smoldering. She put a 60-second spot together and went on the air live at 9 o'clock.

"At that point I called NPR to see if they needed something from me because I had a feeling that everyone at WNYC was either scrambling to get out of the building or to get to the site. I had some distance and was more available," she said.

She then called NPR in Washington, DC. "NPR said they were going to put me on the air with Bob Edwards, host of Morning Edition, in about 10 minutes and to find out what I could." Nolan finally made connections with a WNYC news producer. "I just asked, 'Where do you want me to go and what do you want me to do? I'm on my way into the city.'"

But before she could make a move, the second plane hit the tower. "I'm watching this plane on television, talking to my producer. Apparently the impact and explosion shook our building. All I heard on the other end of the phone was 'Oh, my God! Oh, my God!' Then the phone line went dead."

She called NPR back to tell them what she knew. "They said they were going to put me on the air live with Bob Edwards. 'He'll ask you questions. Just tell him what you've seen. Tell him what you've heard.'"

She reported, "We don't know if this is a terrorist attack. We can make assumptions that it is either that or that something has gone horribly wrong with the air traffic control system." She described the smoke and flames she could observe from her own front door, reporting that the FBI was investigating a possible hijacking. She also said firefighters likely would be unable to put out a fire so high up, probably at about the 85th floor. "This is going to be a long, hard day for people in New York," she concluded.

From there, she said, "It just became a race to see how much information we could get, how quickly we could get it, and then disseminate it."

The Towers Are Coming Down

By this time Beth Fertig was headed toward the towers. "I go running down the street, and I'm pushing through this crowd of thousands of people standing in the middle of Park Place alongside City Hall Park just staring at the towers burning. I heard from a news truck parked along the street that the Pentagon was hit. By this time, I'd figured out that it was terrorism, but I didn't know it was beyond New York."

She remembers pushing through the crowd and looking up at the southern tower that "looked like a candle melting." She noticed that the building was getting a little shorter because the flames were eating it away.

Fertig made it to the southern edge of City Hall Park's traffic circle, two blocks north and one block east of the World Trade Center complex. The buildings were looming above her. She was looking up at the tower when she was stopped by a policewoman who firmly told her, "I can't let you get any closer. We're telling people to turn away."

Feeling the urgency of getting information, Fertig indignantly showed the police officer her press pass and her microphone. "I've got to get there. The mayor is there. I've *got* to get there! I've *got* to cover this!" she insisted. Unmoved, the officer said, "I can't let you go. I'm doing this to protect your life. We don't know what is going to happen next."

Fertig said as if on cue the tower came down. "I hear this huge rumbling noise like an elevated train above my head. I'm staring at this in disbelief. I just held my microphone out to get the sound of it, and, after a few seconds, started narrating what I'm seeing. 'The building is falling, people are running, there's smoke' ... whatever was happening, I just started narrating. Then, I realized, 'Oh, my God, everybody is running.'" She decided to run, too. She just didn't know which direction to go because she couldn't tell which direction the building was likely to fall.

Miraculously, the buildings did one thing that day that saved the lives of many journalists, police and others who were running away from the area. "It just descended like a timed implosion—like when they are deliberately bringing a building down. It was the strangest thing to see. It was coming down so perfectly that in one part of my brain I was thinking, 'They got everyone out, and they're bringing the building down because they have to.'"

Thick, brown smoke was pouring out and rushing east toward her. "The wind was blowing, and the canyons of Lower Manhattan were sucking it. I didn't know where the stuff was blowing, so I knew I'd better run."

For the first time, she thought her life was in danger. "Previously, we were in this suspended state of disbelief, just watching it," she said. She ran north alongside of City Hall Park. "People were running like in a disaster movie. This one man was completely inarticulate. He was just shouting, 'Oh, my God.' He couldn't even speak he was so upset. I kept trying to get him to talk to me, but he was just unable to speak." Then, she thought she didn't really have the time to speak to anyone; she'd better keep running. "I was bumping into emergency vehicles, dodging police who were telling everybody to go north, to go east."

Unknown to Fertig, just prior to the collapse, Amy Eddings also was moving closer to the towers, looking for the plane and someone official to interpret what was going on. It dawned on her that none of the firefighters and emergency medical technicians knew any more than she did. The people who did know were walking past her, leaving the scene. "I starting interviewing people asking, 'What did you see? What do you know?'"

Three men told her they saw at least ten people jump from the towers. "And they hit the ground and there was a loud explosion," one man said. "I was in a conference room in Number 4 World Trade Center, and I couldn't believe my eyes. At first I thought they were, like, stuffed animals or something. But then I saw them waving their hands

... ladies, men." Another man said cars parked along Liberty Street were exploding. One man told her he ran down 73 flights of stairs in the South Tower.

"We saw lights flicker, and then a ton of debris came over the side, and then smoke ... and then the smell of aviation fuel," he told her. He was soaking wet with sweat. Another man thought only one plane had plowed through both buildings. Two women said they came from the 36th floor of the South Tower, the second one hit. "Our lights flickered, and then there was flying debris, and then the building shook," one said. "Everyone said, 'Bomb!,' so we just ran."

When Eddings stood looking up at the North Tower, she could see the mark of the wing where it had sliced into the building. She just wondered, "How in the heck are the firefighters going to get the fire out?"

She walked to a nearby pay phone across the street from Number 4 World Trade Center, with a clear view of the north faces of both towers. "Remember, my cell phone was out," she said. "I thought I could describe the scene for the station. I was basically standing at the bottom looking up at the building." She made a phone call to her newsroom, but no one answered. The building, about seven blocks from the World Trade Center complex, was being evacuated.

She called the NPR news desk in Washington, D.C., at about 9:30 a.m., was asked what new information she had and asked to describe the scene. "I saw the building burning and a huge, gapping hole. People were leaving. Papers were fluttering in the air. The plane had completely disappeared into the building."

Eddings was being patched through to the news program *Morning Edition* to go on the air when a plain-clothes policeman flashed a badge at her and asked her to relinquish the pay phone. She flashed her press credentials and said as firmly as she could, "I'm filing a story." But he was "a big brass guy" who ordered her to "get off the phone right now" for "security" reasons. She reluctantly yielded the phone.

Eddings spent the next ten minutes going from corner to corner trying to find a pay phone. Moving farther north, she ran into a shoeshine store and offered a man $20 to use his phone. But his cell phone battery had died from others who had made the same request. She couldn't find another cell phone or pay phone. "I was running out of options. I was about six blocks away from WNYC. My instinct was to get this on the air ... just get what you have on the air."

She decided to run back in the Municipal Building, schlepping her equipment and her fiancé's wedding shoes. "Waves of people were coming out of the building. A security officer told me the building was being evacuated, and I couldn't go in." At that moment, Laura Walker, president and CEO of WNYC, appeared, and told the guard Amy was coming with her, back to the station's offices. There, they joined Mitch Heskell, vice president of finance, and her fiancé, Mark, who had slipped back upstairs, despite the evacuation order and had continued broadcasting. "We stared at each other and asked, 'Now what?'"

They debated. "We knew this was a big story, and we should be covering it," Eddings said. "But there were rumors being broadcast of more planes in the air. I had even heard a detective on the street, near the towers, telling people to get out of the area because another plane was headed our way—and we didn't know if our building was safe." The consensus was that WNYC listeners and NPR in Washington needed help to get the complete story. They decided to stay in the studio and keep broadcasting. Laura Walker was able to prevent their evacuation.

It was inconceivable to everyone that the towers would fall, Eddings said. "No one, we knew, had factored in the effect of all that jet fuel and the size of the planes." The WNYC building shook and she heard a rumble, but she said it didn't immediately register that a tower was collapsing. "I was numb. It was really hard to break through the denial. It was a good thing because it helped me keep working." The enormity of what had happened didn't hit her until two days later, when she had a chance to watch video images of the collapse.

What Do We Do Now?

When the North Tower collapsed, WNYC's antenna was destroyed along with its FM signal. Several local television and radio stations in New York were suddenly off the air. WNYC was able to continue broadcasting on its sister station's AM frequency through a telephone line linking the station to an AM transmitter in New Jersey. Engineers from NPR hauled a satellite dish to New Jersey to help the station continue to broadcast and to get reports back to NPR's Washington, D.C., studios.

WNYC was able to stay on the air from the studio until around 6 p.m. After that, Mark Hilan handed over the reins to WNYC broadcasters who were now based at NPR's New York Bureau office, about 40 blocks uptown from WNYC's evacuated building.

Fertig found fellow reporter, Marianne McCune, outside of WNYC's building. "All I remember was hugging her and saying, 'Don't go there. I just came back. I saw it all.'" The two women started walking away from the towers, hugging and crying. "It must have been a really strange sight because here are these two reporters holding their microphones and just crying."

Then both women realized they had a job to do.

"Marianne calmed me down and told me to turn on my tape recorder and just narrate what I saw again." They started walking toward Foley Square, just north of their office building, where all the courthouses and the Federal Building are located. They tried to call the station. Although Fertig's cell phone wasn't working, miraculously, McCune's was. "She got through to Mark Hilan who threw me on the air. I started saying, 'I saw it all. This is what I saw. And I played some of my tape. I put my headphone up near the phone and tried to play the tape." Then McCune started pulling witnesses to the phone. She found a man who had seen it all, including people falling from the building. He described what he saw while the building was still burning.

"We stood there together doing this and helping each other because we were both so freaked out. We were really helping each other get through this and coming up with ideas. What do we do as reporters?"

While they were on the air, the second building collapsed. "Mark had us on the air, and I was saying, 'What's that sound?' and Marianne was saying, 'The building is coming down.' Right before it came down, he asked me to describe what I was seeing. I said, 'I can't see the first building. It's come down apparently. But the second building is getting shorter. In retrospect, it made sense what I was seeing. We did that for a while, and then we went to interview other witnesses. We interviewed five fire marshals. We interviewed some office workers who fled the 83rd floor."

She said, "It was a really strange experience because you don't want to be traumatizing people more, but we wanted to get their stories on the air."

Another woman who was comforting two women who fled the Port Authority told them they should talk to these reporters because if their names are on the air, their families will know that they are okay. "So, we did that for a while. When we lost cell phone power, we went into the Department of Health Building where we noticed they were setting up a triage center on the ground floor with doctors and nurses helping people who were mildly injured. The woman who ran the press office let us use her office so that we could get back on the air and tell Mark and NPR what was happening."

After a while, they decided McCune would stay downtown and continue doing interviews. All public transportation had been stopped.

Someone at the Health Department told her where the mayor was, so she walked about forty blocks to find the mayor at his new makeshift command center at the Police Academy on 20th Street where he was beginning to give news conferences. Fertig worked through the night. She did a feature for NPR based on taped interviews she and McCune had done, just recounting the experience of being at Ground Zero.

Fertig forced herself back into the usual newsroom routine, making calls and taking care of administrative duties. Other WNYC reporters were able to get through and were going on the air. There were decisions to make. When she was pulling sound bites from her tape, she ran across the one from the man describing bodies falling. "It was pretty graphic," she said. "I could cut it so it was less graphic. But we decided we wanted to paint an accurate picture of what was going on. We used it in its entirety. As time went on and the story developed, as it shifted into a different stage about the rescue efforts, rather than the attacks themselves, we no longer used that cut. Our coverage changed accordingly."

Nolan soon realized that she wouldn't be able to get into the city that day. "Since I couldn't get in, my job became covering the people who had escaped. Commuter ferries and local fishing vessels were pressed into service and brought people into the harbor in my hometown. A triage unit had been set up right down the street from me, and I was talking to people and watching them come off these boats just covered in ash and shell-shocked."

The people arriving were first seen by medical personnel, and if it was determined they didn't need further treatment, they were taken to a tent where they essentially were hosed down because "Nobody knew what this ash contained. Everyone assumed it was asbestos." She covered these events the rest of the day and into the night.

Eddings and Mark Hilan didn't want to leave the WNYC studios at all the night of September 11. "We slept in the Green Room overnight."

The Morning After

The morning of September 12 brought some relaxation in travel restrictions, and Nolan was able to take a train to Newark and then another train to upper Manhattan. The subways were running. "The city was remarkably normal from Midtown north. If you didn't know something had happened, you would think it was a Sunday just because there was no traffic. I was able to get around fairly easily. I was real surprised at that." Later in the week she was able to take a ferry service between the foot of Wall Street and her home. She said she wasn't hassled and was allowed to walk where she wanted because she had press credentials.

Nolan reunited with her newsroom colleagues, and they all "hit the streets." Armed with a notebook, a minidisk recorder and a cell phone, she spent the next two days going back and forth to various hospitals. "It was very chilling when you heard medical people say, 'We were ready ... we had the triage unit set up ... we waited ... and *nobody* came.' That was their moment of truth. Ordering more body bags was what they were going to have to do. These people who were trained to save lives could do nothing.

"That was the saddest thing to me—to be at the hospitals and just watch them have all this stuff set up in the street ready to take people in and nobody came," Nolan said. "I think they only pulled five survivors out after the towers fell."

Sadly, the failure of some of those inside the building to grasp the enormity of the impact resulted in fewer people getting out. "There were people who were told everything's fine, go back to your desks. And a lot of people did that," Nolan said. "The fact that planes hit at roughly the 80th to 85th floors meant there were 20 floors above that and no one was going to get out. That would be Windows on the World and Cantor Fitzgerald, Aon Corporation, and all the other companies on the top floors of the towers. People on the 15th floor thought, 'We've lost the top half of the building, but we're okay.' *Nobody* anticipated those buildings coming down."

Then the story direction began to change. "Once we realized that the first wave of horror was over, it then became: 'How is the city responding? How is the city reacting—in different communities, the medical community, the arts community, the religious community?'" The WNYC reporters fanned out to get those stories.

"I was chasing down stories that were surfacing," Nolan said. "There were so many false leads. There was at one point a report that under the rubble they had found an SUV with six firefighters inside alive." Confusion reigned about which hospital the firefighters had been taken to. "I went to Bellevue Medical Center, and everyone there who was in some position of authority confirmed everything—yes, this is what we are waiting for. I went to a news conference where the CEO of the hospital said they had been put on alert. He went into a very medical description of why you couldn't just yank these men out of the vehicle and bring them to the hospital and how this was going to take a long time."

Nolan reported the story on the air for WNYC and NPR, using her cell phone. The whole thing was a hoax.

This story is but one illustration of the confusion and misinformation surrounding coverage in those first days. "There were so many people speaking for the city—for the police and the fire department. They hadn't quite coordinated any kind of pressroom yet. The mayor's Office of Emergency Management had been at Number 7 World Trade Center, and that building collapsed. So, it was a matter of finding a place where the press could get information. Those first two days we really didn't have a place like that. There were just so many wild goose chases," she said.

Coping with the Aftermath

Working was difficult in the aftermath, as well. "The air smelled horrible," Nolan said. "It was very acrid like burning wires. We're all convinced we will have lung cancer in ten years."

She was at the Stock Exchange on September 17, the day Wall Street reopened. The air was still very thick. She had to wear a surgical mask—although she said it didn't make much difference—and her eyes stung. She noted with irony that even though the air was "thick enough to cut with a knife," she saw several people walking past her on their way to work smoking. "I thought, 'Why bother? Breathe deep. Here were these thin women in their Chanel suits going back into the Stock Exchange, sucking on their cigarettes. It was so bizarre. It was the first thing we could laugh at."

Eddings experienced what she calls a "curious form of survivors' guilt" causing her to relive those days over and over and ask herself questions with no answers. "How could I have stayed down there longer? What if I'd gone left instead of right? Were there more people I could have interviewed if only I'd stayed near the towers longer? It's 'woulda, shoulda, coulda.'" Her self-struggles come down to whether she could have reported more, reported better or helped more people.

Eddings said she learned from her experience. "Two months later, I covered the crash of American Airlines Flight 587, in the Belle Harbor neighborhood of Queens. I sneaked past checkpoints by hiding in the back of a van filled with volunteer firefighters, and I got within a block of the crash site by ducking under police barricades when officers weren't looking, and cutting through people's backyards."

In spite of her second-guessing about her World Trade Center coverage, she believes WNYC staff members ended up being exactly where they needed to be. "Several of my colleagues were outside, interviewing survivors and rescue workers, while we were inside the station, assisting the anchor." As a team, they were able to cover the story and keep their station on the air in spite of extremely difficult conditions. No reporters were injured. "It really worked out fine," she said. Everything worked out fine except her wedding which had to be postponed until January 2002.

Nolan had never been through anything like this before. She admitted that she was afraid initially when it became obvious that a terrorist attack had occurred so close to home. "All the fear went, and I was able to focus when I heard that all the airports had been shut down and the air space secured. I thought, 'Okay, nobody can come overhead and get me now. That's cool.'"

She said that was when she had to choose what to do next. "I had to go in and tell some stories and just record it," she decided.

Getting on the subway still gives her a twinge, she said, because New Yorkers have realized how vulnerable the subway system could be to attack. But, that doesn't stop her.

"For some reason you have this idea that nothing will happen to you because you're observing it. You're reporting on it. Of course, nothing is going to happen to you. Don't even think about that. You have this idea that there is a bubble of safety around you. Otherwise you wouldn't do it."

"This was an extraordinary moment. I hope I never go through anything like it again. The thing that just amazed me the most is that our news team just hit the streets and came back with amazing, amazing work. I am so proud to be working with these people and so proud that I work at WNYC. I've never before been involved in anything like this. It made me very, very glad that I do what I do," Nolan said.

All the WNYC reporters spent the next several days in a state of high emotional and physical activity. "As a reporter you get this perverse adrenaline. When something horrible happens, you just go into high gear. You look at each other and just go, 'Isn't this amazing? Isn't this incredible?' Everybody was high on adrenaline for days," she said.

But, there was the inevitable letdown after the first days had passed. WNYC had trauma counselors available on the Sunday following the attacks. But, Nolan said she and some of the others were feeling like it was too soon to process it. "Don't ask me to process this yet. If I have to sit down quietly and think about it, I'm not going back out. It was disturbing for a lot of people to have to acknowledge all of it." Although she acknowledged that it was useful in some respects for some people, "For me it was way too early to start thinking about it."

But she did have her moment a couple of days after September 11 when she returned home for the first time. "When I got home, my husband handed me a glass of wine, and I went out and sat on the front porch and just cried my eyes out. It was the first time I had done it. I think I'm not alone in that. Once you had a chance to catch your breath, just the enormity of it overwhelms you. It's huger than you can imagine. On a clear day, I can look out my front door and see Lower Manhattan. I still look at it and go, 'Oh, my God. They're gone. They're *just gone.*' I still can't wrap my mind around this."

Fertig had a similar reaction. When she finally could head for home at 4:30 a.m. on September 12, she couldn't take a taxi, so she had to walk from 14th Street, about a mile to her home. "That was the worst experience of my life. I was walking home alone in the dark, looking toward the Twin Towers. They were gone. It was just the saddest thing in the world."

In the following days, some of their shock gave way to a more tangible emotion: anger. "All of us became really angry." Nolan said. "We feel very protective toward New York. It became very clear that we are all so in love with this place. There's nothing else like it on the planet. In the history of human civilization there has never been a city like New York—not Rome, not Athens, not Alexandria. *How dare they do this to our city!"*

10

Different Functions:
Television and Newspapers*

Xigen Li and Ralph Izard

Within seconds after a plane crashed into the North Tower of the World Trade Center in New York at 8:45 a.m. EST on September 11, 2001, the television networks jumped into action. Even with limited information at the time, news announcers began describing the events that initially they didn't understand. They had no choice, no time to prepare. Newspapers and magazines did have some limited time, and they immediately began planning and reporting for their accounts of the same events to be published the following morning or later.

It was like presenting an extemporaneous speech on a subject of no familiarity. But it was journalism on a massive and immediate scale, and journalists did what they had to do to gain needed information and, as best they could, explain that information to a shocked and dismayed public around the country and the world.

Scholars over the years have devoted much attention to how the news media cover such extraordinary crisis situations.[1] These have dealt with a multitude of different events—acts of terrorism and war, natural disaster, industrial accidents, criminal acts—but they share the fact that they were events that created far-reaching public fear.

---

* The original version of this study appeared in *Newspaper Research Journal,* Vol. 24, No. 1, Winter 2003, pg. 204-218. It is presented here with permission from *Newspaper Research Journal.*

Not surprisingly, researchers found information was the central focus of television coverage, but this information was presented in ways that produced two other results. It changed viewer's understanding or interpretation of events and evoked emotions.[2] Furthermore, they learned that what journalism does during a rapidly moving crisis depends somewhat on how much time has evolved (called "stages"). Initially, the media focus on describing the facts of what happened and, in some instances, help coordinate the relief work. Then they move to making sense of the situation and, ultimately, to place the crisis in a larger, longer-term perspective.[3]

But television and newspapers, even though they share these functions, do not always approach such stories in precisely the same ways. This content analysis of the first twenty-four hours of coverage by five networks and the next day's coverage of eight national newspapers[4] seeks to determine how the competitive advantages and different tasks of newspapers and television in reporting may lead to different coverage patterns of a crisis situation. The September 11 tragedy offers an opportunity to deal with important questions of whether the magnitude of the event and the different print and broadcast work patterns have impact on news content, coverage, and use of sources.

The coverage of 9/11 brought unprecedented challenges to journalists who had no time for advanced preparations and, indeed, even little time to adequately think through the alternatives. This was especially true of television, forced into immediate focus, but newspapers had only a few hours to determine how to deal with the catastrophic events of that day. They were forced to make difficult decisions on the fly, and they organized the news stories as the events unfolded.

Some of those decisions reflect the nature of the two media, perhaps provide early clues of differences and even some of the reasons for the specifics of the coverage. For example, most of the newspaper stories were written by staff reporters (83 percent). A small portion (4.5 percent) was from *The Associated Press*, and the rest were from other sources. Twenty-three percent of the newspaper stories were filed from the World Trade Center, compared to 38 percent by television networks. Eighteen percent of the newspaper stories were filed from the Pentagon, compared to 9 percent of television's coverage. The newspapers carried 6 percent international stories, while networks had 3 percent international stories. Nearly half of the newspaper stories were initiated from other U.S. locations, while 42 percent of network stories were initiated from their studios.

Disaster and Politics the Major Coverage Topics

The findings of this study, indeed, confirm that, in spite of some similarities dictated by traditional journalistic expectations and the nature of the event, newspapers and television networks did demonstrate some different patterns to their coverage. Among the similarities, three stand out as notable—coverage that emphasizes description of the disaster itself, seeking broader understanding about the obvious political implications, and, to a lesser degree, discussion of matters involving public safety.

Specifically, nearly half of the TV stories focused on the disaster itself (44 percent), with political coverage ranking second at 22 percent. These, likewise, were the top categories of newspaper coverage, with each comprising 23 percent of the print coverage. Public safety, at 14 percent, ranked third in the newspaper coverage and (at 9 percent) ranked fourth on the network presentations.

Beyond these, however, newspapers and television networks often deviated. Newspapers, facing the need to go beyond what already had been covered hour by hour by the networks and with more time to prepare, placed greater emphasis on human interest (12 percent) and the economy (10 percent), while networks paid relatively little attention to these topics. On the other hand, the networks made much more use of stories about crime (12 percent) as their third most-used category, while newspapers placed less emphasis (5 percent) on the criminal category.

Newspapers' focus on human interest stories perhaps provides a working example of how newspaper and television journalists do their jobs in a crisis situation such as this. The 9/11 tragedy involved thousands, even millions, of human beings—including more than 3,000 citizens, police officers, firefighters, and paramedics who lost their lives. It directly affected unknown thousands of other people who were injured, displaced or otherwise significantly inconvenienced, and thousands of witnesses who had stories to tell. This human element makes coverage of 9/11 a natural for human interest coverage, a fact confirmed by both media for months after the attacks.

But at the time of the attacks, television broadcast live throughout the first twenty-four hours and beyond. It worked to keep the public immediately informed of what was happening and, eventually, what was behind the scenes. In those early hours, the networks' priority on informing the public—actually covering the events of the crisis—exceeded the urge to develop more human-interest stories. The results of this study indicate clearly that television's human interest coverage was an evident highlight only during the later stage of their coverage on that first day.

Thus, the contrast becomes apparent between newspapers' 12 percent and television's 4 percent of stories dedicated to the more human and personal elements of the tragedy. Among the eight newspapers in this study, all except the *Los Angeles Times* had more than 10 percent of stories framed as human interest. Except for ABC (5 percent), all networks had less than 5 percent of stories in this category.

In fact, among the newspapers, the *Los Angeles Times*—across the country and four time zones away—provided many of the few examples of the few differences in coverage patterns among newspapers. Its location provided even greater opportunity for planning and seeking information, and it thus had fewer stories devoted primarily to describing the disaster (10 percent) and more on the economy and human interest.

Among the networks, NBC separated itself from the others in several ways. Nearly half of the total coverage by the networks collectively stressed disaster (44 percent), but NBC provided proportionately more disaster stories (54 percent). CNN had the largest number of political stories (26 percent), while CBS had 16 percent. In addition, NBC devoted much more attention to issues of safety.

While all networks had stories framed as safety (around 8 percent), NBC had 18 percent in this category. In addition, NBC had fewer stories highlighting crime (5 percent) as compared to the collective network coverage that ranged from 12 percent to 18 percent. NBC also was much lower in human-interest stories (1 percent), compared to 4 percent of the networks collectively.

In the chaos of trying to cover the events of the day, neither newspapers nor television devoted attention to one function listed frequently by scholars—that of serving as a source of guidance and consolation to the public. Television provided such guidance 1.8 percent of the time, compared to newspapers' 1.6 percent.

Further, in attempting to deal with this very complicated situation, information was the primary goal for both media. More newspaper stories (86 percent) were primarily factual than those of the networks (76 percent). In general, network coverage (19 percent) offered more analysis than newspapers (9 percent).

Relying on Government Sources during Times of Crisis

As is often the case, reporting during the early hours of 9/11 reconfirmed the journalistic tendency—print and broadcast—to call first on government sources. Even though the patterns of source use were considerably different between the two media, government sources were dominant in overall coverage of both the newspapers (40 percent) and television networks (18 percent). Six of eight newspapers used government officials in more than 40 percent of their stories.

And it should not be surprising under the circumstances that newspaper sources overall were more diversified than those of the networks. Following government officials, the only noticeable sources used by networks were witnesses of the incident (10.5 percent), experts (4.3 percent) and the president (2.6 percent). A much larger range of sources was used by newspapers, including witnesses (34 percent), business (28 percent), experts (23 percent), international (13 percent) and the president (12 percent).

Aside from simply answering the question of who had opportunities to speak or whose viewpoints were dominant, source selection also is meaningful because sources relate to types of coverage. Government sources strongly dominated (66 percent) the newspapers' political coverage, followed distantly by witnesses, business, experts, international and the president. Likewise, human-interest stories involved witnesses 57 percent of the time as their major sources, and experts were used extensively in the stories that stressed the economy (46 percent) and criminal (70 percent).

Newspaper stories that focused on descriptions of the disaster relied on witnesses as their major sources (70 percent), with government officials (41 percent) second. International sources were cited in criminal (41 percent) and political (23 percent) stories. Sources cited in the stories about safety were business (37 percent) and government officials (35 percent).

Similar relationships were determined for the television networks. Overall, the most frequently used sources were government officials, witnesses, and experts. The political category associated mostly with government sources (36.2 percent), the disaster stories used witnesses (20.3 percent) and government officials (10.3 percent), criminal and terrorism stories used government officials (18.8 percent) and experts (17.3 percent), and stories about safety used government officials (16.9 percent) and airline officials (7.5 percent).

The differences in sources used by newspapers and networks may be attributed to the nature of the system, the competitive advantages and reporting styles of each medium. A variety of sources simply is easier to achieve in print stories with more time available and without television's visual emphasis. Television's dominant form in covering 9/11 involved reporting on the spot, and this resulted in less use of quoted sources.

Television's Role Changed as the Day Progressed

Since the television networks were forced to provide immediate information, their roles evolved as the day progressed, and the stage of coverage played an important role. Not surprisingly, in the immediate aftermath of the planes crashing into the towers (that is, during the first stage, from 8:45 to 11 a.m.), network coverage was single-mindedly devoted to describing the disaster (56.8 percent). A few other stories were devoted to political (14.7 percent), criminal and terrorism (12.5 percent), and safety concerns (8.9 percent).

During the second stage, from 11 a.m. to 3 p.m., television took advantage of some planning time and greater opportunities to research broader issues. Thus, coverage that focused directly on the disaster (37.2 percent) declined, while political stories (28.7 percent) and safety stories (10.8 percent) increased. Criminal and terrorism stories (11.7 percent) remained the same.

After 3 p.m., stories framed as disaster (31.5 percent) continued to decline, and it was at this point that human interest coverage (10.9 percent) increased noticeably. Political content (22.6 percent) remained high, and safety (7.1 percent) stayed at the same level as in the previous two stages. Broader issues, such as the economy (2.5 percent) and the environment (3.7 percent) became more evident.

Same Event, Different Functions

The complexity of the circumstances facing journalists on 9/11 cannot be overstated. With no prior knowledge, they were plunged into the midst of a national chaos that had never before been faced in this country. And both television and newspapers responded, first by emphasizing the principal expectation of journalism—providing information and describing what happened.

The five television networks and eight newspapers in this study first placed their emphasis on providing as much specific information as they knew about what happened. Then, when possible, they moved on to broader implications of the circumstances facing the nation and the world. In the first eight hours of television coverage and in the first newspaper issues on September 12, both media primarily provided factual information. They sought to inform, explain, and interpret the events and serve as vital sources for public knowledge and understanding.

Beyond that, however, television and the newspapers demonstrated their different perspectives—indeed, their differing functions—on how to deal with the events and issues of the day. Television has the competitive advantage of immediacy, and therefore focused during the first eight hours on description, often playing the TV trump card of providing compelling graphic visuals. As the day progressed, they increased their access to sources and began to deal with the broader implications of the attacks.

Newspapers the next day started at the same place by describing, perhaps even in greater detail, the events themselves and their political implications. But they used the time available to dig more deeply. TV already had informed a shattered nation of what physically had happened. It was up to newspapers to concentrate on explanations and implications of those events. They could, and did, interview a wider variety of sources, particularly officials, experts, and non-official citizens. They could focus more on human-interest stories about how the tragedies affected people's lives, and they could develop the political, economic, and international elements of the story.

So, of course, they're different. They're supposed to be. Television is there first; it's visual and now. Newspapers follow, reiterate what happened, and provide explanation. Each medium works with what it has and what it is. From the perspective of American citizens, therefore, they are complementary, and the combination of the two provided the American people—indeed, the world—with as much basis for understanding as may have been possible under the circumstances.

Notes

1.   See, for example, Nacos, B. (1994). *Terrorism and the Media: From the Iran Hostage Crisis to the Oklahoma City Bombing*. New York: Columbia University Press; Chiasson Jr., L. (1995) (Ed.): *The Press in Times of Crisis*. Westport, CN: Praeger.; Caldwell, J.T. (1995). *Televisuality, Style, Crisis and Authority in American Television*. New Brunswick, NJ: Rutgers University Press; Altheide, D.L. (2002). *Creating Fear: News and the Construction of Crisis*. New York: Aldine de Gruyter.
2.   Graber, D. A. (1980). *Mass Media and American Politics*. Washington, DC: *Congressional Quarterly Press*.
3.   See, for example, Johnson, T. J., & Boudreau, T. (1996). Turning the Spotlight Inward: How Five Leading News Organizations Covered the Media in the 1992 Presidential Election, *Journalism & Mass Communication Quarterly*, 73 (3), pg. 657-671; Delli Carpini, M. X., & Williams, B. A. (1984). Terrorism and the Media: Patterns of Occurrence and Presentation, 1969-1980. In H. H. Han (Ed.): *Terrorism, Political Violence and World Order* (pg. 103-134). New York: University Press of America; Semetko, H. A., & Valkenburg, P. M. (2000). Framing European Politics: A Content Analysis of Press and Television News, *Journal of Communication*, 50 (2), pg. 93-109.
4.   Included in this study were five television networks (ABC, CBS, NBC, CNN and FOX News) and eight national newspapers (The *New York Times, Washington*

Post, *Los Angeles Times*, *Milwaukee Journal Sentinel*, *Denver Post*, *St. Louis Post-Dispatch*, *Houston Chronicle* and *Atlanta Journal and Constitution*).

11

Public Response:
Crisis and Presidential Approval*

Jennifer Kowalewski

The source is lost in antiquity, but the quote is not.

"I don't care what you say about me, as long as you say something about me, and as long as you spell my name right."

Some attribute it to George M. Cohen, the famed showman, others to former President Harry S. Truman, and others still to sources as diverse as Louisiana Sen. Huey P. Long and famed circus magnate P.T. Barnum. But no modern-day president is likely to repeat it—or to believe it.

For they understand that the nature of society, especially its political system, today has changed. What the media say about you is critical—and no one knows that better than former President George W. Bush, who saw his rating soar through the roof after favorable media reaction to 9/11—and plunge into the watery depths four years later when the media turned against him after Hurricane Katrina.

And the effect is even more pronounced when citizens are glued to television—and when they think the media are doing a good job of reporting.

In spite of evidence that public attitudes about the media have been in decline, the importance of 9/11 and the Gulf Coast hurricanes clearly led to desperate searches for information. Americans spent hours watching and reading in the aftermath of the terrorist attacks, according to

* This study is based on Kowalewski's master's thesis at the E.W. Scripps School of Journalism, Ohio University.

the Pew Research Center, with 81 percent saying they were constantly tuned in to news reports, and 63 percent reporting they were "addicted" to the coverage.[1]

Further, a WestGroup Research telephone survey one day after the attack found that the public "overwhelmingly" approved the television coverage, and a survey by Pew Research Center from September 13-17, 2001, found "unprecedented" positive reaction (89 percent) to media coverage.

And the public's approval of the media's coverage mirrored the ups and downs of President Bush's approval—and disapproval—during his two terms in office.

The president saw his approval ratings swell following the terrorist attacks of September 11, 2001, when he led the nation through and beyond the devastating assaults in New York, Washington, and an isolated field in Pennsylvania. As the nation stood frozen in the debris of the attacks, people united behind his administration. The news media did likewise.

Yet, just four years later, support for the commander-in-chief eroded. It is likely that growing disapproval of the war in Iraq and investigations that erupted over governmental ethics and secrecy were prominent. But a contributing factor—if not the primary factor because of the immediacy of media coverage—was the federal government's failures during and following the storms of August 2005 when hurricanes Katrina and Rita devastated the Gulf Coast region.

For days, it was unbelievable that the Federal Emergency Management Agency (FEMA), which had undergone changes since September 11, could not get organized to provide assistance but, at the same time, insisted that help was on the way. But for citizens the buck stopped at the top, and journalists began asking why with direct, even angry, questions of the Bush administration.

Does a relationship exist between how the public reacts to its political leaders and a supportive, even acquiescent, media or, alternatively, a critical and questioning journalism? Many scholars think so.

Maxwell McCombs and Donald Shaw, for example, found when the media increased their coverage of issues, the public cited those issues as more pressing in their own lives. In fact, they said, "the media are the major primary sources of national political information: for most, mass media provide the best—and only—easily available approximation of ever-changing political realities."[2]

The researchers believed such agenda setting had two levels. First, the media determine the agenda. Then, they influenced public opinion through opinion leaders who judged issues as important or not. Researchers discovered that "specific attributes of a topic" influence public opinion.[3] News outlets kept some information out of the public view, while placing other information into their coverage. The media, therefore, influenced how people perceived a politician based on what was written or broadcast.[4]

This study investigates the association between public approval ratings of the president and his administration in the Gallup Poll and whether coverage was critical, neutral, or supportive (the "tone" of the coverage) in fifteen of the nation's largest newspapers from 2001 through 2005.[5] Determination of tone was based on analysis of the first five paragraphs of each story.

Impact of the Terrorist Attacks

Prior to the attacks of September 11, 2001, public approval ratings of the president as reported by the Gallup Poll, were stagnant. President Bush came to the White House after defeating Vice President Albert Gore in the swing state of Florida to win the contested 2000 presidential race. Thus, he arrived in the midst of controversy.[6] The Gallup Poll rating of the president hovered in the 50 percent range at the beginning of his presidency. Newspaper supportive tone remained near 30 percent.

Everything changed, however, that blue-skied morning of September 11. The United States had an enemy—Osama bin Laden—and President Bush vowed to get him "dead or alive."[7] A week after the attack, on September 19, President Bush visited what became known as ground zero, the debris of the collapsed World Trade Center in New York City. He stood atop the rubble of the Twin Towers and yelled into the bull-horn—"the rest of the world hears you, and the people who knocked these buildings down will hear all of us soon"—amid chants of "U.S.A.! U.S.A.! U.S.A.!"[8]

On October 7, less than one month after the terrorist attacks, President Bush ordered the invasion of Afghanistan to root out the Taliban-led government, which supported the al-Qaeda terrorist network and the al-Qaeda leader bin Laden himself. Saying it was an effort to protect the nation, Bush asked Congress for expanded power to fight terrorism at home.

Congress responded quickly by passing the United and Strengthening America by Providing Appropriate Tools Required to Intercept and Obstruct Terrorism Act, better known as the USA Patriot Act, on October 26. The Patriot Act provided a broad array of law-enforcement powers without court approval, including "roving wiretaps, far-reaching powers to search a home or office and the ability to hold non-citizens for seven days without specified charges."[9]

Following the terrorist attacks, Gallup Poll numbers indicate that the president's job approval rating soared to a high of 88 percent in October 2001, then settled into the 70 percent range, momentarily making him one of the most popular presidents in U.S. history.[10]

Parallel to the increasing Gallup Poll numbers, the media's supportive tone in news stories rose sharply. One editorial from the Washington Post rounded up 2001, writing, "President Bush has been converted from the hesitant partisan he seemed to many before Sept. 11 into a broadly accepted symbol of national unity and a reliable wartime commander in chief, whose judgment is reinforced by an exceptionally strong national security team."[11]

In this study's investigation of the one year following the devastating attack, the tone of newspaper coverage significantly correlated with the Gallup Poll. The numbers of critical, supportive, and neutral statements following the terrorist attacks indicated that newspapers in general became less critical and more neutral.

One month before the attack, the supportive newspaper tone was 28.6 percent. In September 2001, newspapers articles were 46.6 percent supportive and 37.9 percent neutral. By the following month, the number of supportive articles decreased to 38 percent, while the number of neutral articles rose to 51.2 percent. It is interesting to note that the number of critical statements fell from 15.5 percent in September to 10.9 percent in October. By the end of the time period, January 2002, as Figure 11.1 indicates, newspapers had the largest number of critical statements at 24.2 percent, with both supporting and neutral statements at 37.9 percent.

Meanwhile, President Bush's popularity, as reflected in the Gallup Poll, increased even more rapidly. The Gallup Poll approval rating increased almost immediately following the terrorist attacks to 88 percent in October compared to 76 percent in September and 56 percent in August. Following the peak, the approval rating of the president decreased slightly, to 77 percent in November 2001, before rebounding to 86 percent in December and 84 percent in January.

Among individual newspapers, the *San Francisco Chronicle* provides a significant example of the correlation between news coverage and the Gallup Poll results. The *Chronicle*'s support of Bush increased immediately after the attacks, then paralleled the

Figure 11.1

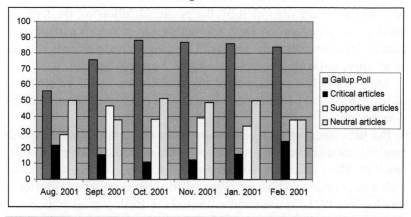

Note: Tone of all the newspapers combined compared with the Gallup Poll approval rating for the six months surrounding the September 11, 2001, attacks

Gallup Poll numbers. In November, the newspaper had no articles critical of the president, 66.7 percent supportive and 33.3 percent neutral. The other newspapers had a positive relationship with the Gallup Poll approval rating, but the results were not as notable.

Impact of Hurricanes Katrina and Rita

As his second term began on January 20, 2005, President Bush's approval rating had begun to plummet. At the time, the approval rating was 52 percent, but fell into the 40 percent range by April.[12]

Certainly, any assessment of the impact of hurricanes Katrina and Rita on the president's public approval ratings is complicated because of a snowstorm of issues in late 2005 that attracted ongoing media and public criticism.

One clearly was Bush's Oct. 3 nomination of unknown jurist Harriet Miers to replace Sandra Day O'Connor on the U.S. Supreme Court, a move that sparked a backlash even from conservatives within his own party.

Another issue—controversy and a subsequent investigation of the 2003 release of CIA operative Valerie Plame's identity to the media—fed the downward spiral. The case involved several administration officials and resulted in the vice president's former chief of staff, I. Lewis "Scooter" Libby, being indicted and found guilty of lying to investigators, although his thirty-month prison sentence eventually was commuted by President Bush.

Within months, the country also learned of a secret domestic eaves-dropping program supported by the president following the terrorist attacks four years earlier. Bush had authorized monitoring of international telephone calls and e-mails of U.S. citizens and residents without court-approved warrants, the *Washington Post* reported.[13]

And, clearly and perhaps most important, debate over the invasion of Iraq became and continued to be a crucial point of public and media discussion.

But the context of such controversy does not diminish the impact of massive criticism of the government's response to hurricanes Katrina and Rita. Many saw the administration's response as totally inadequate, including, curiously, those who investigated the September 11 terrorist attacks. The 9/11 Commission criticized the Bush administration and Congress for "minimal progress" in making changes to domestic policy to handle disasters.[14]

Two weeks after the hurricanes on the Gulf Coast, Bush accepted responsibility for the federal government's failing, and FEMA Director Michael Brown resigned. Nearly a month following the devastation, local and state officials claimed "red tape and poor planning have left thousands of evacuees without basic services."[15]

With the controversies of late 2005, the president's approval rating fell even lower. In October 2005, the Gallup Poll reported President Bush's approval rating dropped to 41 percent. In November, public approval fell to 38 percent, followed by a slight rebound in December, to 42 percent.[16]

When Katrina and Rita struck the Gulf Coast, newspaper coverage shifted to a critical tone almost instantly. A month later, the Gallup Poll showed the public followed suit. Although the results were not significant at this point, the correlation was positive. The study looked at six months surrounding Katrina, including one month prior, in July 2005, through December 2005. In July and August 2005, newspapers had more supportive articles in print, 31.3 percent and 30.8 percent respectively, compared to 20.8 percent and 28.2 percent critical. But both were eclipsed by the number of neutral, at 41 percent.

By September 2005, the number of critical articles had jumped to 53.9 percent, with only 9 percent supportive and 37.2 percent neutral. As the time period continued, the number of critical articles decreased, while the number of supportive articles increased slightly and the number of neutral stories increased to 50 percent in both November and December 2005. As shown in Figure 11.2, critical articles went from 31.5 percent to 33.3 percent, while the number of supportive articles decreased from 18.5 percent in November to 16.7 percent in December.

Note, though, that the Gallup Poll approval rating decreased more slowly than newspaper support, when compared month-by-month. Prior to the hurricanes, the Gallup Poll reported the approval rating at 47 percent in July 2005. In August and September, Gallup Poll approval rating remained the same, at 44 percent, dropping in October to 41 percent. The Gallup Poll continued to decrease at the same pace as the newspaper coverage to 38 percent in November and 32 percent in December.

Within individual newspapers, none correlated significantly with the Gallup Poll approval rating when compared month-by-month. However, a pattern is indicated when one notes that the newspapers became more critical more quickly than what was reflected by the Gallup Poll approval rating. The highest level of newspaper criticism occurred immediately after the storms, in September, as the ineptitude of the federal assistance mechanisms became increasingly apparent. Thereafter, the newspapers moved into a more neutral mode for the next three months even as the Gallup Poll was indicating a continued high level of public dissatisfaction.

Relationship between Coverage and Presidential Approval

Following the attacks of September 11, 2001, newspapers did increase their supportive tone, while decreasing the number of critical articles in

Figure 11.2

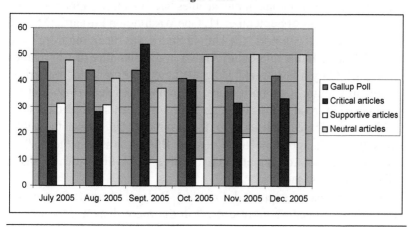

Note: Tone of all the newspapers combined compared with the Gallup Poll approval rating for six months surrounding Hurricane Katrina

print. However, focus was more on neutral articles in the aftermath of September 11. The media focused on coverage about what the administration needed to do to stop another terrorist attack. Even if articles had critical comments, these were countered with supportive statements, making them more neutral in tone.

For example, one *New York Times* article discussed how the Bush administration had agreed to give New York City more money than originally promised to begin rebuilding in the aftermath. But the article made clear "the announcement did not satisfy some members of New York's Congressional delegation who have been increasingly concerned that the White House would renege on its initial promise."[17]

In another article, the newspaper questioned the administration's policy of withholding presidential papers, even if a previous president wanted them made public. Following a president leaving office, papers of a former president should be released twelve years after that president's departure. Bush's executive order left papers of former President Ronald Reagan private, despite a court order to release them.

"Critics have accused the current administration of trying to withhold documents that might be embarrassing not only to the president's father, but to other administration officials who served Mr. Reagan," the *Times* said. "Among them are Secretary of State Colin L. Powell; Mitchell E. Daniels Jr., the budget director; and Lawrence B. Lindsey, the chief White House economist."[18] But the newspaper balanced those critical statements with supportive comments from others who favored the president's policies.

Despite the neutral tone, many articles became more supportive after the terrorist attacks of September 11. One Washington Post article talked about the "positive support" the United States was receiving from leaders in Pakistan, India, and Saudi Arabia in the planning of war against terrorism.[19] Only a few weeks later, the newspaper reported bipartisan support in Congress, as politicians, including President Bush and his administration, rose to the challenge following the terrorist attacks.

"The nation's elected leaders for the past month have given the public precisely the 'changed tone' that President Bush promised in the election a year ago but proved scarcely able to deliver in his first nine months in office,"[20] the *Post* said.

But the increased support did not last. It should be noted the newspapers did not become more critical in the more distant aftermath of the terrorist attack; rather, by one month after the attack, the media did question what the government would do to ensure the safety of the nation. The results should not be surprising in light of traditional statements of newspaper neutrality and adherence to the fairness and balance concepts taught in newsrooms and journalism schools. Yet, it is clear that newspapers did become more supportive of the president and his administration in the aftermath of September 11.

The opposite could be said after the devastation of hurricanes Katrina and Rita. As people clamored for help, newspapers questioned the government's response to the natural disaster. Immediately following the disaster, the *San Francisco Chronicle* criticized the "the Republican-led Congress and President Bush" for responding to the hurricanes "by throwing open the taxpayers' checkbooks" with $62.3 billion appropriated for Katrina relief.

The newspaper went on to speak with former U.S. Attorney General Edwin Meese, chairman of the Center for Legal and Judicial Studies at the Heritage Foundation, who said "overreacting in Washington usually means throwing money at the problem. We want to be fiscally responsible."[21]

In another article, the *Chronicle* reported "it is a measure of how far off course his presidency has strayed that President Bush spent nearly an hour discussing his priorities with reporters Tuesday and hardly brought up Iraq, Social Security or taxes."[22]

The *New York Times* discussed the Democratic leaders who "unleashed a burst of attacks" on President Bush and his administration, "saying the wreckage in New Orleans raised doubts about the country's readiness to endure a terrorist attack and exposed ominous economic rifts they said had worsened under five years of Republican rule."[23] Democrats in Congress, as well as the Democratic National Committee chairman, questioned the leadership of the president in the weeks after Hurricane Katrina devastated the Gulf Coast and flooded New Orleans. Nearly a month before the Gallup Poll approval rating decreased, newspapers already questioned the administration's leadership in the aftermath of this natural disaster.

One interesting point may be noted with the lag time between all of the newspapers' tone compared to the Gallup Poll approval rating. It took one month for the Gallup Poll approval rating to decline in what may have been response to media coverage. Researchers have determined it takes time for an agenda to permeate to society. James P. Winter and Chaim P. Eyal said, "The optimal effect span is four- to six-week period" showing "recent media emphasis rather than cumulative effects over time" will lead "to public salience."[24] In the aftermath of Hurricane

Katrina, it took the public overall nearly five weeks to become more critical of the president, indicating a relationship between the coverage in the newspapers and the Gallup Poll approval rating.

What the study showed was although newspaper coverage became more supportive following September 11, the media became more neutral and less critical as well. But after five years of the Bush administration, the newspaper support, and the Gallup Poll approval rating, waned dramatically. After hurricanes Katrina and Rita, problems in the administration's handling of the disaster showed in news coverage across the country. As more questions were raised by the media regarding the relief efforts, the Gallup Poll approval rating decreased.

Concurrent with other controversial issues, Hurricane Katrina opened the floodgates of criticism of the Bush administration. In the aftermath, newspaper coverage continued its persistent criticism of the president, and the Gallup Poll continued to report low approval ratings, having dropped to 32 percent in June 2007.[25] The relationship between the Gallup Poll and newspaper coverage thus continued to haunt the Bush administration. Thus, it remains clear that the printed word still affects public opinion.

Notes

1.   Pew Research Center (2001, September 19). "American Psyche Reeling from Terror Attacks," press release. Retrieved on July 2, 2007, from http://people-press. org/reports/display.php3?ReportID=3.
2.   McCombs, M., & Shaw, D. (1972). "The Agenda-Setting Function of Mass Media," *Public Opinion Quarterly*, 32, Pg. 185.
3.   McLeod, D.,Kosicki,G., & McLeod, J. (2002). "Resurveying the Boundaries of Political Communication Effects." In J. Bryant & D. Zillman (Eds.): *Media effects: Advances in theory and research* (pp. 227). Mahwah, New Jersey: Lawrence Erlbaum Associates, Inc.
4.   McCombs, M., & Reynolds, A. (2002). "News Influence on Our Pictures of the World." In J. Bryant & D. Zillman (Eds.): *Media Effects: Advances in Theory and Research* (pp. 10). Mahwah, New Jersey: Lawrence Erlbaum Associates, Inc.
5.   The newspapers included in the study are *Cleveland Plain Dealer, Minneapolis Star Tribune, St. Louis Post Dispatch, New York Times, Philadelphia Inquirer, Washington Post, Atlanta Journal Constitution, Dallas Morning News, St. Petersburg Times, Arizona Republic, Denver Post, Las Vegas Review Journal, Los Angeles Times, San Francisco Chronicle,* and *Seattle Times.*
6.   Bumiller, E., & Bruni, F. (2001, September 19). "A Nation Challenged: The President; In Crisis, Bush Writing His Own Script," The *New York Times,* Pg. B11.
7.   Bumiller, E., & Bruni, F. (2001, September 19). "A Nation Challenged: The President; In Crisis, Bush Writing His Own Script," The *New York Times,* Pg. B11.
8.   McFadden, R. (2001, September 15). "After the Attacks; The President; Bush Leads Prayer, Visits Crews; Congress Backs Use of Armed Force," The *New York Times,* Pg. A1.

9.   McGee, J. (2001, November 4). "An Intelligence Giant in the Making: Anti-Terrorism Law Likely to Bring Domestic Apparatus of Unprecedented Scope," *Washington Post*, Pg. A4.
10. The Gallup Organization, Princeton, N.J. Retrieved on June 15, 2006, from http://www.gallup.com.
11. Broder, D.S. (2001, December 26). "Triumphs of 2001," *Washington Post*, Pg. A31.
12. Gallup Poll.
13. Eggen, D. (2005, December 31). "Justice Department Investigating Leak of NSA Wiretapping; Probe Seeks Source of Classified Data," *Washington Post*, Pg. A1.
14. Shenon, P. (2005, September 15). "Storm and Crisis: Commission Criticizes Storm Response," *New York Times*, Pg. A23.
15. Vedantam, S., & Starkman, D. (2005, September 18). "Lack of Cohesion Bedevils Recovery; Red Tape, Lapse in Planning Stall Relief," *Washington Post*, Pg. A1.
16. Gallup Poll.
17. Hernandez, R. (2001, November 2). "A Nation Challenged: Federal Aid; New York May Get More Than Bush Promised," *New York Times*, Pg. B10.
18. Bumiller, E. (2001, November 2). "Bush Keeps a Grip on Presidential Papers," *New York Times*, Pg. A22.
19. Harris, J. F. (2001, September 17). "Bush Gets More International Support for U.S. 'Crusades' Against Terrorism; Officials Warn New Attacks Are Possible," *Washington Post*, Pg. A1.
20. Balz, D., & Harris, J.F. (2001, October 14). "Shock of War May Have Changed the Tone in Politics; As Polls Find Public Confidence in Government Soaring, Leaders Seem to Rise to the Occasion with Bipartisan Effort," *Washington Post*, Pg. A3.
21. Epstein, E. (2005, September 14). "Conservatives Question Spending; Their Relief Plan Urges Reallocating Pork, Lowering Taxes, Rolling Back Regulations," *San Francisco Chronicle*, Pg. A10.
22. Sandalow, M. (2005, October 5). "Bush Defends Miers from his Own; News Analysis; Katrina, Gas Prices, Iraq Violence have Pushed President Off Course," *San Francisco Chronicle*, Pg. A1.
23. Nagourney, A., & Hulse, C. (2005, September 8). "Democrats Intensify Criticism of White House Response to Crisis," *New York Times*, Pg. A21.
24. Winter, J. P, & Eyal, C. P. (1981). "Agenda Setting for the Civil Rights Issue," *Public Opinion Quarterly* 45, Pg. 381.
25. Gallup Poll.

References

Alali, A.O., & Eke, K.K. (1991). *Media Coverage of Terrorism: Methods of Diffusion.* Newbury Park, CA: Sage Publications.

Alexander, Y. (1978). Terrorism, the Media, and the Police. *Journal of International Affairs, 32*(1), 101-114.

Altheide, D. L. (2002). *Creating Fear: News and the Construction of Crisis.* New York: Aldine de Gruyter.

Altschull, H. (1984). *Agents of Power: The Role of the News Media in Human Affairs.* New York: Longman.

American Society of Newspaper Editors. (1999). *Examining Our Credibility: Perspectives of the Public and the Press.* Reston, VA: American Society of Newspaper Editors.

Apple, W., & Hecht, K. (1982). Speaking Emotionally: The Relation between Verbal and Vocal Communication of Affect. *Journal of Personality and Social Psychology, 42*, 864-875.

Argyle, M., Alkema, F., & Gilmour, R. (1971). The Communication of Friendly and Hostile Attitudes by Verbal and Nonverbal Signals. *European Journal of Social Psychology, 1*, 385-402.

Atwater, T. (1989). News Format in Network Evening News Coverage of the TWA Hijacking. *Journal of Broadcasting & Electronic Media, 33*(3), 293-304.

Atwater, T. (1990). Network Evening Coverage of the TWA Hostage Crisis. In A. Yonah & R. Latter (Eds.). *Terrorism and the Media: Dilemmas for Government, Journalists, and the Public.* (pp. 63-72). New York: Brassey's Inc.

Babad, E. (1999). Preferential Treatment in Television Interviewing: Evidence from Nonverbal Behavior. *Political Communication, 16*, 337-358.

Babad, E., Bernieri, F., & Rosenthal, R. (1989). Nonverbal Communication Leakage in the Behavior of Biased and Unbiased Teachers. *Journal of Personality and Social Psychology, 56*, 89-94.

Balz, D., & Harris, J. F. (October 14, 2001). Shock of War May Have Changed the Tone in Politics; As Polls Find Public Confidence in Government Soaring, Leaders Seem To Rise To the Occasion with Bipartisan Effort. *The Washington Post*, p. A3.

Baraka, A. (September 17, 2001). Somebody Blew up America. *Broadcasting & Cable.* Retrieved March 23, 2007, from *http://www.amiribaraka.com/blew.html.*

Blair, T. (June 12, 2007). Lecture by the Prime Minister, The Right Honorable Tony Blair, MP, on public life. Retrieved on April 13, 2008, from *http://image.guardian.co.uk/sys-files/Politics/documents/2007/06/12/BlairReustersSpeech.pdf.*

Broadcasting & Cable. (September 17, 2001). New York: Reed Business Information.

Broder, D. S. (December 26, 2001). Triumphs of 2001. *The Washington Post*, p. A31.

Buck, R., & VanLear, C. A. (2002). Verbal and Nonverbal Communication: Distinguishing Symbolic, Spontaneous, and Pseudo-Spontaneous Nonverbal Behavior. *Journal of Communication, 52*(3), 522-541.

Bumiller, E. (November 2, 2001). Bush Keeps a Grip on Presidential Papers. *The New York Times*, p. A22.

Bumiller, E., & Bruni, F. (September 19, 2001). A Nation Challenged: The President; In Crisis, Bush Writing His Own Script. *The New York Times*, p. B11.

Burgoon, J. K., Birk, T., & Pfau, M. (1990). Nonverbal Behaviors, Persuasion, and Credibility. *Human Communication Research, 17*(1),140-169.

Caldwell, J. T. (1995). *Televisuality, Style, Crisis and Authority in American Television.* New Brunswick, NJ: Rutgers University Press.

Campbell, C. P. (1995). *Race, Myth, and the News.* Thousand Oaks, CA: Sage.

Campbell, D. (1993). Cold Wars: Securing Identity, Identifying Danger. In F. M. Dolan & T. L. Dumm (Eds.). *Rhetorical Republic: Governing Representations in American Politics* (pp 39-60). Amherst, MA: University of Massachusetts Press.

CBS News. (2002). *What We Saw: The Events of September 11, 2001–In Words, Pictures, and Video.* New York: Simon & Schuster.

Chiasson, L., Jr. (Ed.). (1995). *The Press in Times of Crisis.* Westport, CT: Praeger.

Cleland, G. L., & Ostroff, D. H. (1988). Satellite News Gathering and News Department Operations. *Journalism Quarterly, 65,* 946-951.

CNN (September 15, 2001). *Saturday Morning News: America's New War* [Television broadcast]. New York: Cable News Network. Retrieved April 13, 2008, from *http:// transcripts.cnn.com/TRANSCRIPTS/0109/15/smn.19.html.*

CNN Transcript (September 11, 2001) Retrieved September 22, 2001, from www.cnn. com.

Coleman, R. (2003). Race and Ethical Reasoning: The Importance of Race to Journalistic Decision Making. *Journalism & Mass Communication Quarterly, 80*(2), 295-310.

Collins, S., & Long, A. (2003). Too Tired To Care? The Psychological Effects of Working with Trauma. *Journal of Psychiatric & Mental Health Nursing, 10*(1), 17-27.

Commission on Freedom of the Press. (1946). *A Free and Responsible Press: A General Report on Mass Communication: Newspapers, Radio, Motion Pictures, Magazines, and Books.* Chicago: The University of Chicago Press.

Cozma, R. (2005). Risk Communication: The Importance of Source Diversity to Credible and Interesting Reporting. Unpublished master's thesis, Louisiana State University, Baton Rouge, LA.

Craft, S., & Wanta W. (2004). Women in the Newsroom: Influences of Female Editors and Reporters on the News Agenda. *Journalism & Mass Communication Quarterly, 81*(1), 124-138.

Crelisten, R. D. (1997). Television and Terrorism: Implications for Crisis Management and Policy-Making. *Terrorism and Political Violence, 9*(4), 8-32.

Day, L. A. (2002). *Ethics in Media Communications: Cases & Controversies.* Belmont, CA: Thomson Learning.

de Zengotita, T. (April 2002). The Numbing of the American Mind: Culture as Anesthetic. *Harper's Magazine.* Retrieved September 8, 2007, from *http://www.csubak. edu/~mault/Numbing% 20of%20american%20mind.htm.*

Delli Carpini, M. X., & Williams, B. A. (1984). Terrorism and the Media: Patterns of Occurrence and Presentation, 1969-1980. In H. H. Han (Ed.). *Terrorism, Political Violence and World Order* (pp. 103-134). New York: University Press of America.

DePaulo, B. M. (1992). Nonverbal Behavior and Self-Presentation. *Psychological Bulletin, 111*(2), 203-243.

Dominick, J. R. (1996). *The Dynamics of Mass Communication.* New York: McGraw-Hill.

Domke, D., Garland, P., Billeaubeaux, A., & Hutcheson, J. (2003). Insights into U.S. Racial Hierarchy: Racial Profiling, News Sources, and September 11. *Journal of Communication, 5,* 606-623.

Duckworth, D. H. (1991). Facilitating Recovery from Disaster-Work Experiences. *British Journal of Guidance and Counselling, 19*(1), 13-22.

Dunsmore, B. (1996). *The Next War: Live?* Cambridge: Harvard University Press.

Easterbrook, G. (November 5, 2001). Free Speech Doesn't Come without Cost. *The Wall Street Journal*, p. A20.

Edinger, J. A., & Patterson, M. L. (1983). Nonverbal Involvement and Social Control. *Psychological Bulletin, 93*, 30-56.

Editorial (September 5, 2002). Death, Destruction, Charity, Salvation, War, Money, Real Estate, Spouses, Babies, and Other September 11 Statistics. *New York Magazine*. Retrieved on March 31, 2008, from *http://nymag.com/news/articles/ wtc/1year/ numbers.htm.*

Eggen, D. (December 31, 2005). Justice Department Investigating Leak of NSA Wiretapping: Probe Seeks Source of Classified Data. *The Washington Post*, p. A1.

Ekman, P. (Ed.). (1983). *Emotion in the Human Face* (2nd ed.). New York: Cambridge University Press.

Ekman, P., & Friesen, W. V. (1975). *Unmasking the Face*. Englewood Cliffs, NJ: Prentice-Hall.

Electronic Frontier Foundation. (2003). The USA Patriot Act, Electronic Frontier Foundation. Retrieved March 20, 2008, from http://w2.eff.org/patriot/.

Elliott, D. (2004). Terrorism, Global Journalism, and the Myth of the Nation State. *Journal of Mass Media Ethics*, 19(1), (pp. 29-45).

Englis, B. G. (1994). The Role of Affect in Political Advertising: Voter Emotional Responses To the Nonverbal Behavior of Politicians. In M. C. Eddie T. C. Brock, & D. W. Stewart (Eds.). *Attention, Attitude and Affect in Response to Advertising* (pp. 223-247). Hillsdale, NJ: Lawrence Erlbaum.

Engstrom, E., & Ferri, A. (2000). Looking through a Gendered Lens: Local U.S. Television News Anchors' Perceived Career Barriers. *Journal of Broadcasting & Electronic Media, 44*(4), 614.

Entman, R. M. (1990). Modern Racism and the Images of Blacks in Local Television news. *Critical Studies in Mass Communication, 7*, 332-345.

Entman, R. M. (1991). Framing U.S. Coverage of International News: Contrasts in Narratives of the KAL and Iran Air Incidents, *Journal of Communication, 41*, 6-27.

Entman, R. M., & Rojecki, A. (2000). *The Black Image in the White Mind*. Chicago: University of Chicago Press.

Epstein, E. (September 14, 2005). Conservatives Question Spending: Their Relief Plan Urges Reallocating Pork, Lowering Taxes, Rolling Back Regulations. *San Francisco Chronicle*, p. A10.

Friedman, H. S., Mertz, T. I., & DiMatteo, M. R. (1980). Perceived Bias in the Facial Expressions of Television News Broadcasters, *Journal of Communication, 30*, 103-111.

Gabler, N. (October 9, 2005). Good Night, and the Good Fight. *New York Times*, 12.

The Gallup Organization, Retrieved June 15, 2006, from *http://www.gallup.com.*

Gamson, W., Croteau, D., Hoynes, W., & Sasson, T. (1992). Media Images and the Social Construction of Reality. *Annual Review of Sociology, 18*, 373-393.

Gamson, W. A., & Modigliana, A. (1993). The Changing Culture of Affirmative Action. *Research in Political Sociology, 3*, 137-177.

Gasser, H.P. (2002). Acts of Terror, 'Terrorism' and International Humanitarian Law, *International Review of the Red Cross, 84*, 547-570.

Graber, D. A. (1980). *Mass Media and American Politics*. Washington, DC: Congressional Quarterly Press.

Graber, D. A. (1988). *Processing the News: How People Tame the Information Tide*. White Plains, New York: Longman.

Graber, D. A. (1990). Seeing in Remembering: How Visuals Contribute to Learning from Television News. *Journal of Communication, 40*(3), 134-155.

Greenberg, B. S., Hofshire, L., & Lachlan, K. (2002). Diffusion, Media Use and Interpersonal Communication Behaviors. In B.S. Greenberg (Ed.), *Communication and Terrorism: Public and Media Responses to 9/11* (pp. 3-16). Cresskill, NJ: Hampton Press.

Grusin, E. K., & Utt, S. (Eds.) (2005). *Media in an American Crisis: Studies of September 11, 2001.* New York: University Press of America, Inc.

Hackett, R. A. (1984). Decline of a Paradigm? Bias and Objectivity in News Media Studies. In M. Gurevitch & M. R. Levy (Eds.), *Mass Communication Review Yearbook: Vol. 5* (pp. 251-274). Beverly Hills, CA: Sage.

Haley, R. L., Richardson, J., & Baldwin, B. M. (1984). The Effects of Nonverbal Communication in Television Advertising. *Journal of Advertising Research, 24,* 11-18.

Hall, J. A. (1984). *Nonverbal Sex Differences: Communication Accuracy and Expressive Style.* Baltimore/London: Johns Hopkins University Press.

Hamilton, J. M., & Krimsky, G. A. (1996). *Hold the Press: The Inside Story on Newspapers,* Baton Rouge, LA: Louisiana State University Press.

Hansson, S. O. (2001). *The Structure of Values and Norms,* Cambridge, MA: Cambridge University Press.

Harris, J. F. (September 17, 2001). Bush Gets More International Support for U.S. 'Crusades' against Terrorism; Officials Warn New Attacks are Possible. *Washington Post,* Pg. A1.

Haynes, M. (December 22, 2006). A Tragedy's Emotional Impact Can Engulf Journalists. *Pittsburgh Post-Gazette,* E1.

Hernandez, R. (November 2, 2001). A Nation Challenged: Federal Aid; New York May Get More than Bush Promised. *The New York Times,* p. B10.

Hersh , S. (September 17, 1985). Speech to journalism students, Louisiana State University.

Iyengar, S. (1989). How Citizens Think about National Issues: A Matter of Responsibility. *American Journal of Political Science, 33,* 878-900.

Iyengar, S. (1991). *Is Anyone Responsible? How Television Frames Political Issues.* Chicago: University of Chicago Press.

Iyengar, S., & Kinder, D. R. (1987). *News that Matters.* Chicago: University of Chicago Press.

Iyengar, S., & Simon, A. (1993). News Coverage of the Gulf Crisis and Public Opinion: A Study of Agenda-Setting, Priming, and Framing. *Communication Research, 20*(1), 365-383.

Izard, C. E. (1977). *Human Emotions.* New York: Plenum Press.

Janik, A. S. (1994). Professional Ethics 'Applies' Nothing. In H. Pauer-Studer (Ed.), *Norms, Values and Society* (pp. 197-204). Vienna Circle Institute Yearbook, Dordrecht: Kluwer Academic Publishers.

Johnson, T. J., & Boudreau, T., (1996). Turning the Spotlight Inward: How Five Leading News Organizations Covered the Media in the 1992 Presidential Election. *Journalism & Mass Communication Quarterly, 73*(3), 657-671

Johnson T., & Kaye, B. (2004). Wag the Blog: How Reliance on Traditional Media and the Internet Influence Credibility Perceptions of Weblogs among Blog Users. *Journalism & Mass Communication Quarterly 81*(3), 622-642. Retrieved July 2, 2007 from Communication & Mass Media Complete.

Kanihan, S. F., & Gale, K. L. (2003). Within 3 Hours, 97 Percent Learn about 9/11 Attacks. *Newspaper Research Journal, 24*(1), 78-91.

Keinan, G., Sadeh, A., & Rosen, S. (2003). Attitudes and Reactions to Media Coverage of Terrorist Acts. *Journal of Community Psychology, 31,* 149-166.

Kellner, D. (2006). September 11, Social Theory, and Democratic Politics. In A. P. Kavoori & T. Fraley (Eds.). *Media, Terrorism, and Theory* (pp. 161-178). Oxford: Rowman & Litlefield Publishers.

Kinsley, M. (April 7, 2006). The Twilight of Objectivity; Lou Dobbs Might Be a Bit Overheated but the New Media Direction is Clear. *Pittsburgh Post Gazette*, B7.

Li, X. (2005). Stages of Crisis and Media Frames and Functions: U.S. Television Coverage of the 9/11 Incident during the First 24 Hours. Paper presented at the annual conference of International Communication Association, New York.

Li, X. and Izard, R. (2005). 9/11 TV, Newspapers Coverage Reveals Similarities, Differences. In E.K. Grusin, & S.H. Utt (Eds.). *Media in an American crisis: Studies of September 11, 2001* (pp. 89-103). New York: University Press of America, Inc.

Liebler, C., & Smith, S. (1997). Tracking Gender Differences: A Comparative Analysis of Network Correspondents and Their Sources. *Journal of Broadcasting & Electronic Media, 41*(1), 58-61.

Lowrey, W. (2004). Media Dependency during a Large-Scale social disruption: The case of September 11. *Mass Communication and Society*, 7 (3), 339-357.

McCombs, M., & Reynolds, A. (2002). News nfluence on our pictures of the world. In J. Bryant & D. Zillman (Eds.). *Media effects: Advances in theory and research* (pp. 10). Mahwah, New Jersey: Lawrence Erlbaum Associates, Inc.

McCombs, M., & Shaw, D. (1972). The Agenda-Setting Function of Mass Media, *Public Opinion Quarterly, 32*, 185.

McFadden, R. (September 15, 2001). After the Attacks; The President; Bush Leads Prayer, Visits Crews; Congress Backs Use of Armed Force, *The New York Times*, p. A1.

McGee, J. (November 4, 2001). An Intelligence Giant in the Making: Anti Terrorism Law Likely to Bring Domestic Apparatus of Unprecedented Scope. *The Washington Post*, A4.

McHugo, G. J., Lanzetta, J. T., Sullivan, D. G., Masters, R. D., & Englis, B. G. (1985). Emotional Reactions to a Political Leader's Expressive Displays. *Journal of Personality and Social Psychology, 49*(6), 1513-1529.

McLeod, D., Kosicki, G., & McLeod, J. (2002). Resurveying the Boundaries of Political Communication Effects. In J. Bryant & D. Zillmann (Eds.), *Media Effects: Advances in Theory and Research*, (p. 227). Mahwah, NJ: Lawrence Erlbaum Associates.

McNair, B. (2007). UK Media Coverage of September 11. In T. Pludowski (Ed.), *How the World's News Media Reacted to 9/11: Essays from around the Globe* (pp. 30-38). Spokane, WA: Marquette Books LLG.

The Media Institute. (1983). *CNN vs. the Networks: Is More News Better News? A Content Analysis of the Cable News Network and the Three Broadcast Networks.* Washington, DC: The Media Institute.

Mehrabian, A. (1968). Inference of Attitudes from the Posture, Orientation, and Distance of a Communicator. *Journal of Consulting and Clinical Psychology, 32*, 296-308.

Merrill, J. C. (1997). *Journalism Ethics: Philosophical Foundations for News Media.* New York: St. Martin's Press.

Meyrowitz, J. (1985). *No Sense of Place: The impact of electronic media on social behavior.* New York: Oxford University Press.

Mindak, W. H., & Hursh, G. D. (1965). Television's Function on the Assassination Weekend. In B. S. Greenberg & E. B. Parker (Eds.), *The Kennedy Assassination and the American Public: Social Communication in Crises*, (pp. 1-25). Stanford, CA: Stanford University Press.

Mogensen, K. (2000). *Arven: Journalistikkens traditioner, normer og begreber* [The heritage: Traditions, Norms and Terms in Journalism]. Copenhagen: Roskilde Universitetsforlag.

Mogensen, K. (2007). How U.S. TV Journalists Talk about Objectivity in 9/11 Coverage. In T. Pludowski (Ed.), *How the World's News Media Reacted to 9/11: Essays from around the Globe,* (pp. 301-318). Spokane, WA: Marquette Books.

Mogensen, K., Lindsay, L., Li, X., Perkins, J., & Beardsley, M. (2002). How TV News Covered the Crisis: The Content of CNN, CBS, ABC, NBC and Fox. In B.S. Greenberg (Ed.), *Communication and Terrorism: Public and Media Responses to 9/11,* (pp. 101-120). Cresskill, NJ: Hampton Press.

Moriarty, S. E., & Garramone, G. M. (1986). A Study of Newsmagazine Photographs of the 1984 Presidential Campaign, *Journalism Quarterly, 63*(4), 728-734.

Moriarty, S. E., & Popovich, M. N. (1991). Newsmagazine Visuals and the 1988 Presidential Election, *Journalism Quarterly, 68*(3), 371-380.

Mullen, B., Futrell, D., Stairs, D., Tice, D. M., Baumeister, R. F., Dawson, K. E., et al. (1986). Newscasters' Facial Expressions and Voting Behavior of Viewers: Can a Smile Elect a President? *Journal of Personality and Social Psychology, 52*(2), 291-295.

Mullen, L. (1998). Close-Ups of the President: Photojournalistic Distance from 1945 to 1974. *Visual Communication Quarterly, 53*(4), 4-6.

Murrie, M. (1998). Communication Technology and the Correspondent. In J.S. Foote (Ed.), *Live from the Trenches,* (pp. 94-104). Carbondale, IL: Southern Illinois University Press.

Nacos, B. L. (1994). *Terrorism and the Media: From the Iran Hostage Crisis to the Oklahoma City Bombing.* New York: Columbia University Press.

Nacos, B. L. (1994). *Terrorism and the Media: From the Iran Hostage Crisis to the World Trade Center Bombing.* New York: Columbia University Press.

Nacos, B. L. (2002). *Mass-Mediated Terrorism. The Central Role of the Media in Terrorism and Counterterrorism.* New York: Rowman & Littlefield Publishing Inc.

Nacos, B. L. (2003). Terrorism as Breaking News: Attack on America. *Political Science Quarterly, 118*(1), 23-52.

Nagourney, A., & Hulse, C. (September 8, 2005). Democrats Intensify Criticism of White House Response to Crisis. *The New York Times,* A21.

National Commission on Terrorist Attacks upon the United States. (2004). *9/11 Report.* New York: St. Martin's Paperbacks.

National Research Council Committee on Disasters and the Mass Media. (1980). *Disasters and the Mass Media: Proceedings of the Committee on Disasters and the Mass Media Workshop.* Washington, DC: National Academy of Sciences.

Neal, A. G. (1998). *National Trauma & Collective Memory: Major Events in the American Century.* New York: M. E. Sharpe Inc.

Nimmo, D., & Combs, J. E. (1985). *Nightly Horrors: Crises Coverage in Television Network News.* Knoxville, TN: The University of Tennessee Press.

Nord, L. W., & Stromback, J. (2003). Making Sense of Different Types of Crises: A Study of the Swedish Media Coverage of the Terror Attacks against the United States and the U.S. Attacks in Afghanistan. *Harvard International Journal of Press/Politics, 8*(4), 54-75.

OECD. (2003). Emerging Systemic Risks in the 21st Century: An Agenda for Action, OECD's International Futures Programme. Retrieved July 27, 2006, from *http://www.unisdr.org/eng/ library/Literature/7754.pdf.*

Overholser, G. (2006). On Behalf of Journalism: A Manifesto for Change. Retrieved on September 1, 2007, from *http://www.annenbergpublicpolicycenter.org/Overholser/20061011_JournStudy.pdf.*

Pan, Z., & Kosicki, G. M. (1997). Priming and Media Impact on the Evaluations of the President's Performance. *Communication Research, 24*(1), 3-30.

Pew Research Center for the People & the Press. (September 19, 2001). American Psyche Reeling from Terror Attacks [Press Release]. Retrieved August 22, 2007, from *http://people-press.org/reports/display.php3?ReportID=3.*

Pew Research Center for the People & the Press. (2001, October). Americans Open to Dissenting Views on the War on Terrorism [Press Release]. Retrieved October 22, 2003, from *http://www.people-press.org/reports/display.php3?reportID=3.html.*

Pew Research Center. (March 14, 2006). State of the News Media: Tough Times for Print Journalism—and in-depth reporting. Retrieved on April 13, 2008, from *http://pewresearch.org/ pubs/213/state-of-the-news-media.*

Pfau, M. (1990). A Channel Approach to Television Influence. *Journal of Broadcasting & Electronic Media, 34*(2), 195-214.

Picard, R. G. (1993). *Media Portrayals of Terrorism. Functions and Meaning of News Coverage.* Ames, IA: Iowa State University Press.

Project for Excellence in Journalism with Princeton Survey Research Associates (January 28, 2002). Return to Normalcy? How the Media Have Covered the War on Terrorism [Press Release]. Retrieved August 22, 2007, from *http://www.journalism.org/node/281.*

Reynolds, A., & Barnett, B. (2003). This Just In...How National TV News Handled the Breaking 'Live' Coverage of September 11, *Journalism & Mass Communication Quarterly, 80*(3), 115-119.

Richmond, V. P., McCroskey, J. C., & Payne, S. K. (1991). *Nonverbal Behavior in Interpersonal Interactions.* Englewood Cliffs, NJ: Prentice-Hall.

Robertson, L. (2001). Anchoring the Nation. *American Journalism Review, 23*, 40-45.

Roig-Franzia, M., & Hsu, S. (September 4, 2005). Many Evacuated, but Thousands Still Waiting. *The Washington Post,* A1.

Rosenthal, R., Hall, J., & DiMatteo, M. R., Rogers, P., & Archer, D. (1979). *Sensitivity to Non-Verbal Communication: The PONS Test.* Baltimore, MD: Johns Hopkins University Press.

Ross, A. (1968). *Directives and Norms*, London: Routledge & Kegan Paul.

Sandalow, M. (October 5, 2005). Bush Defends Miers from His Own; News Analysis; Katrina, Gas Prices, Iraq Violence Have Pushed President off Course. *San Francisco Chronicle,* A1.

Schaffert, R. W. (1992). *Media Coverage of Terrorists: A Quantitative Analysis.* New York: Praeger.

Schramm, W. (1965). Communication in Crisis. In B.S. Greenberg & E. B. Parker (Eds.), *The Kennedy Assassination and the American Public: Social Communication in Crises.* Stanford, CA: Stanford University Press.

Schuster, M. A. (2001). A National Survey of Stress Reactions after the September 11, 2001 Terrorist Attacks. *New England Journal of Medicine, 345*(20), 1507-1512.

Seib, P. (2000). *Going Live: Getting the News Right in a Real-Time, Online World.* Lanham, MD: Rowman & Littlefield.

Seipp C. (June 2002). Online Uprising. *American Journalism Review, 24*(5), 42-47.

Semetko, H. A., & Valkenburg, P. (2000). Framing European Politics: A Content Analysis of Press and Television News. *Journal of Communication, 50*(2), 93-109.

September 11 News.com. (2001). *September 11 News Attack Images.* Retrieved April 13, 2008, from *http://www.september11news.com/AttachImages.htm.*

Shenon, P. (September 15, 2005). Storm and Crisis: Commission Criticizes Storm Response, *The New York Times,* A23.

Shoemaker, P. J., & Reese, S. D. (1996). *Mediating the Message: Theories of Influences on Mass Media Content.* New York: Longman.

Smith, T. W., Rasinksi, K. A., & Toce, M. (October 25, 2001). America Rebounds: A National Study of Public Response to the September 11th Terrorist Attacks, The National Opinion Research Center. Retrieved April 13, 2008, from *http://www.norc. uchicago.edu/ projects/reaction/pubresp.pdf.*

Society of Professional Journalists. (2003). Society of Professional Journalists: Code of Ethics. Retrieved April 13, 2008, from *http://www.spj.org/ethicscode.asp.*

Stempel, G., & Hargrove, T. (2002). Media Sources of Information and Attitudes about Terrorism. In B. S. Greenberg (Ed.), *Communication and Terrorism* (pp. 3-16). Cresskill, NJ: Hampton Press.

Stocking, H. S., & Gross, P. H. (1989). How Do Journalists Think: A Proposal for the Study of Cognitive Bias in Newsmaking. *ERIC Document Reproduction Services No. ED309463.* Bloomington, IN: Smith Research Center, Indiana University.

Sullivan, D. G., & Masters, R. D. (1988). Happy Warriors: Leaders' Facial Displays, Viewers' Emotions, and Political Support. *American Journal of Political Science, 32*(2), 345-368.

Sylvester, J., & Huffman, S. (2002). *Women Journalists at Ground Zero: Covering Crisis.* Lanham, MD: Rowman & Littlefield.

Tuggle, C. A., & Huffman, S. (2001). Live Reporting in Television News: Breaking News or Black Holes? *Journal of Broadcasting & Electronic Media, 45*(2), 335-344.

Ungar, S. (March 1998). Hot Crises and Media Reassurance: A Comparison of Emerging Diseases and Ebola Zaire. *The British Journal of Sociology, 49*(1), 36-56.

Vanderbilt University (October 23, 2003). *Vanderbilt University News Archive.* Retrieved April 3, 2002 from *http://tvnews.vanderbilt.edu/.*

Vedantam, S., & Starkman, D. (September 18, 2005). Lack of Cohesion Bedevils Recovery; Red Tape, Lapse in Planning Stall Relief. *The Washington Post,* p. A1.

Wagner, H. L., Buck, R., & Winterbotham, M. (1993). Communication of Specific Emotions: Gender differences in sending accuracy and communication measures. *Journal of Nonverbal Behavior, 17*(1), 29-54.

Weaver, D., Beam, R., Brownlee, B., Voakes, P., & Wilhoit, G. C. (in press). *The American Journalist in the 21ˢᵗ Century.* Mahwah, NJ: Lawrence Erlbaum Associates. Preliminary results can be found at *www.poynter.org/content/content_view. asp? id=28778.*

WestGroup Research. (September 13, 2001). Americans Believe Attack on American TV Coverage Accurate; Anchors Professional [Press Release]. Retrieved October 22, 2003, from http://www.westgroupresearch.com/crisiscoverage/.

Wikipedia. (2007). Amiri Baraka. Retrieved on March 23, 2007, from http://en.wikipedia. org/ wiki/Amiri_Baraka.

Whitney, C., Fritzler, M., Jones, S., Mazzarella, S., & Rakow, L. (1989). Geographic and Source Biases in Network Television News, 1982-1984. *Journal of Broadcasting & Electronic Media, 33*(2), 159-174.

Winter, J. P., & Eyal, C. P. (1981). Agenda Setting for the Civil Rights Issue. *Public Opinion Quarterly, 45,* (Fall), 381.

Woods, K. (August 6, 2002). Handling Race/ethnicity in Descriptions: A Teaching Module. *Poynter Online.* Retrieved April 13, 2008, from *https://www.poynter.org/ content/content_view.asp?id=9518.*

Zelizer, B. & Allan, S. (2002). Introduction: When Trauma Shapes the News, In B. Zelizer & S. Allan (Eds.). *Journalism after September 11* (pp.1-24). New York: Routledge.

Zoch, L. M., & Turk, J. V. (1998). Women Making News: Gender as a Variable in Source Selection and Use. *Journalism & Mass Communication Quarterly, 75,* 762-776.

List of Contributors

Renita Coleman is assistant professor in the School of Journalism, University of Texas at Austin.

Suzanne Huffman is professor and Broadcast Department Head, Texas Christian University.

Ralph Izard is Sig Mickelson/CBS professor in the Manship School and professor emeritus, E.W. Scripps School of Journalism, Ohio University.

Sonora Jha is assistant professor, Department of Communication & Journalism, Seattle University.

Jennifer Kowalewski is assistant professor in the Schieffer School of Journalism at Texas Christian University.

Xigen Li is associate professor, City University of Hong Kong.

Kirsten Mogensen is associate professor, Department of Communication, Business and Information Technologies, Roskilde University, Denmark.

Jay Perkins is associate professor, Manship School of Mass Communication, Louisiana State University.

Judith Sylvester is associate professor, Manship School of Mass Communication, Louisiana State University.

H. Denis Wu is associate professor, College of Communication, Boston University.

List of Interviews*

Andrew Alexander, Cox Newspapers, Washington, April 21, 2006

Emily Atkinson, Editorial Producer, CNN, January 24, 2002

Sharri Berg, Vice President of News Operations, FOX News, February 12, 2002

Steve Capus, Executive Producer, *NBC Nightly News*, March 8, 2002

Gail Chalef, Managing Editor, Network Bookings, CNN, January 24, 2002

Cory Charles, Director, International Guest Bookings, CNN, January 24, 2002

Don Dahler, Correspondent, ABC, March 7, 2002

Robert Dembo, National News, Assignment Desk, NBC, March 8, 2002

Joy E. DiBenedetto, Vice President, Network Bookings, CNN, January 24, 2002

Rosemary Dillard, wife of 9/11 victim Eddie Dillard, March 19, 2003

Amy Eddings, Reporter, WNYC Radio, New York, October 22, 2001

Rehema Ellis, Correspondent, NBC News, CBS, March 7, 2002

Molly Falconer, Business News Correspondent, FOX News, February 12, 2002

Note: Many of these journalists have changed jobs since they were interviewed. They are listed here in the position they held at the time of the interview.)

Bill Felling, National Editor, CBS, March 7, 2002

Tom Fenton, Vice President, Deputy Managing Editor, International News Gathering, CNN, January 24, 2002

Beth Fertig, Reporter, WNYC Radio, New York, November 2, 2001

Paul E. Friedman, Executive Vice President, ABC, March 7, 2002

Steve Friedman, Senior Executive Producer, *The Early Show*, CBS, CBS, March 7, 2002

John Gibson, Anchor, FOX News, February 12, 2002

Lester Holt, Anchor, MSNBC, CBS, March 7, 2002

Brian Kennedy, National Desk, ABC, March 7, 2002

Matt Lauer, Host, *The Today Show*, NBC, March 8, 2002

Keith McAllister, Senior Vice President and National Managing Editor, CNN, January 24, 2002

Marcy McGinnis, Senior Vice President, News Coverage, CBS, CBS, March 7, 2002

Liz Mercure, Supervising Producer, CNN, January 24, 2002

Stephanie Moris, Futures Editor, Network Bookings, CNN, January 24, 2002

Jim Murphy, Executive Producer, *CBS Evening News*, CBS, March 7, 2002

Dennis Murray, Daytime Executive Producer, FOX News, February 12, 2002

Kerry Nolan, Reporter, WNYC Radio, New York, October 17, 2001

Al Ortis, Executive Producer, Special Events, CBS, March 7, 2002

John Roberts, Senior National Correspondent, CNN, April 21, 2006

Michael Rosen, Special Events, ABC, March 7, 2002

Shelley Ross, Executive Producer, *Good Morning America*, ABC, March 7, 2002

Abraham Scott, husband of 9/11 victim Janice Scott, March 19, 2003

Jon Scott, Anchor, Fox News, February 12, 2002

Eric Shaw, Senior Correspondent, FOX News, February 12, 2002

Bill Shine, Network Executive Producer, FOX News, February 12, 2002

Paul Slavin, Executive Producer, *World News Tonight*, ABC, March 7, 2002

Shepard Smith, Anchor, FOX News, February 12, 2002

John Stack, Vice President, Newsgathering, FOX News, February 12, 2002

Gary Tuchman, National Correspondent, CNN, January 24, 2002

Paul Varian, Managing Editor, Newswires, CNN, January 24, 2002

Jonathan Wald, Executive Producer, The Today Show, NBC, March 8, 2002

Bill Wheatly, Vice President, NBC News, March 8, 2002

Brian Williams, Anchor and Managing Editor, *NBC Nightly News*, November 16, 2006

Index

For Product Safety Concerns and Information please contact our EU
representative GPSR@taylorandfrancis.com Taylor & Francis Verlag GmbH,
Kaufingerstraße 24, 80331 München, Germany

Batch number: 08153776

Printed by Printforce, the Netherlands